Signature Tastes ®

www.SignatureTastes.com

Do you remember that place your sister
took us to when we stayed with her last year?

Why yes. Yes we do.

Those restaurant recipes and a whole lot more.
We all remember a great meal...

the *company*, the *place* and the *food*.

About the Author

Steven W. Siler is a firefighter-cum-chef serving in Charleston, South
Carolina. He is the author of several cookbooks of restaurant recipes
from across the nation. In addition, he has served as an editor and
contributing writer for several food publications.

Take your tastebuds for a stroll through
New Orleans' *Signature* restaurants!

www.TastebudTours.com
(219) 929-6648

Brewer's Crabfingers
Abita Brewpub
Abita Springs, LA

2 sticks (16 tablespoons) butter, softened
1/4 cup Worcestershire sauce
1 sprig rosemary
2 tablespoons chopped garlic
Pinch of cayenne pepper, more or less to taste
1 tablespoon black pepper

Juice of half a lemon
Pinch of Cajun or Creole seasoning
2 to 4 dashes Louisiana-style hot sauce
Pinch of paprika
1 pound Louisiana crab fingers
1/2 cup Abita Amber beer

Method:

1. Combine all ingredients except crab fingers and beer in a medium pan and cook over medium heat until butter melts and ingredients blend.

2. Add crab fingers and sauté briefly before adding beer. Simmer to reduce for about 10 or 15 minutes.

3. Serve with hot French bread for dipping into the buttery sauce.

Prohibition had a large effect on music in the United States, specifically jazz, which originated in New Orleans. Speakeasies became far more popular during the prohibition era, partially influencing the mass migration of jazz musicians from New Orleans to major northern cities like Chicago and New York.

Macaroni with Cheddar Velouté and Pulled Pork
American Sector
New Orleans, LA

1 2-pound pork shoulder (Boston butt)
2 tablespoons liquid smoke
1 tablespoon red pepper flakes
Cajun or Creole seasoning, to taste
2 tablespoons olive oil
1 rib celery, small dice
2 onions, small dice
1 carrot, small dice
1 whole garlic bulb, split in half
5 sprigs fresh thyme
1 quart pork stock
Barbecue Sauce (recipe follows)
House-made Macaroni (recipe follows) or 1
pound store-bought macaroni,
cooked to package directions
Cheddar Cheese Sauce (recipe follows)
Crumb Topping (method follows)
chervil springs, for garnish
Barbecue Sauce:
1 cup ketchup
1 onion, diced small
1/2 cup Dijon mustard
1/4 cup apple cider vinegar

1 teaspoon garlic powder
1 teaspoon onion powder
Housemade Macaroni:
2 pounds all-purpose flour
7 eggs
pinch of salt
2 tablespoons water
Cheddar Cheese Sauce:
1 quart heavy cream
1 tablespoon crushed garlic
1 tablespoon diced shallots
1 tablespoon fresh thyme leaves
4 cups shredded cheddar cheese
salt and freshly ground pepper to taste
2 tablespoons sambal olek
1 cup mayonnaise
Crumb Topping:
3 cups panko bread crumbs
1 1/2 cups Parmesan cheese, finely grated
1 tablespoon fresh thyme leaves
1 teaspoon red pepper flakes
2 tablespoons olive oil

1. Rub pork shoulder with the liquid smoke, sprinkle evenly with red pepper flakes and seasoning. Wrap in plastic wrap and let sit, refrigerated, for 12 hours or overnight.

2. Add the olive oil to a sauté pan set over medium-high heat. Add the celery, onions, and carrots and cook until lightly caramelized, about 7 minutes. Add garlic, thyme sprigs, and pork stock. Raise heat to high and bring to a boil. Add the pork shoulder, cover, reduce heat to low, and simmer for 3 hours or until fork tender.

3. Allow to cool. Shred the pork into large chunks with 2 forks. Toss the pork in the barbecue sauce.

4. Preheat oven to 350°F. To assemble, combine the pasta with the barbecue pork mixture.

5. Fold in the cheese sauce. Add the mixture to a shallow casserole dish and top with the crumb crust. Bake until topping is golden brown, about 40 minutes.

Barbecue Sauce:

1. Combine all ingredients and bring to a boil in a saucepan set over high heat.

Housemade Macaroni:

1. Combine the flour, eggs, salt, and water in a mixing bowl. Using a paddle attachment, mix until a smooth dough is achieved. Allow the dough to rest for 10 minutes in the refrigerator before proceeding. The dough may be rolled out by hand or by using a pasta maker (hand or electric.)

2. If using a pasta maker, mix until a flaky dough is achieved. Place macaroni die onto extruder and extrude pasta. Cut noodles into 1 inch lengths as they come out of the extruder. Cook in lightly salted boiling water until al dente, 2 to 3 minutes.

Cheddar Cheese Sauce:

1. In a saucepan set over medium heat, add the cream, garlic, shallots, and thyme. Bring to a simmer and reduce by one fourth. Whisk in the cheddar and season with salt and pepper to taste. Fold in sambal olek (Asian chili sauce) and mayonnaise when you combine with the pasta.

Crumb Topping:

1.Combine all dry ingredients and fold in olive oil.

Peach Melba
Antoine's
New Orleans, LA

6 slices your favorite almond pound cake
3 cups French vanilla ice cream
6 slices fresh Ruston peaches, peeled
1 cup of Melba sauce (raspberry sauce), see recipe below

2/3 cup chopped roasted almonds
Melba Sauce:
3 cups of raspberries
1/4 cup confectioner's sugar
1 tablespoon lemon juice

1. Place a slice of almond pound cake in the bottom of each of six dessert bowls. Top each with a scoop of French vanilla ice cream (about 1/2 cup) and then a fresh peach slice. Pour Melba sauce over peaches and ice cream. Garnish with chopped roasted almonds.

Melba Sauce:

1. Makes approximately 1 cup

2. Purée the raspberries, confectioners' sugar, and lemon juice in a blender. Strain to remove seeds.

Oysters Rockefeller
Antoine's
New Orleans, LA

36 fresh (live) oysters on the half shell
3 tablespoons olive oil
3 tablespoons butter
3 tablespoons finely-minced fresh spinach leaves
1 tablespoon finely-minced capers
3 tablespoons finely-minced watercress
3 tablespoons finely-minced green onions
3 tablespoons finely-minced parsley

5 tablespoons homemade bread crumbs
Tabasco Sauce to taste
1/2 teaspoon Herbsaint
1/2 teaspoon salt
dash of cayenne pepper
½ teaspoon white pepper
Rock Salt
Lemon wedges for garnish

1. Using an oyster knife, pry open the oyster shells, then remove the oysters. Discard the top shells; scrub and dry the bottom shells. Drain the oysters, reserving the oyster liquor.

2. In a large saucepan, melt the butter; add spinach, onion, parsley, bread crumbs, Tabasco Sauce, Herbsaint, and salt. Cook, stirring constantly, for 15 minutes. Remove from heat. Press the spinach mixture through a sieve or food mill; let cool. Mixture may be made ahead of time and refrigerated until ready to use.

3. Preheat oven broiler. Line an ovenproof plate or platter with a layer of rock salt about 1-inch deep (moisten the salt very slightly). Set oysters in the rock salt, making sure they are level.

4. Place a little of the reserved oyster liquor on each oyster. Spoon an equal amount of the prepared spinach mixture over each oyster and spread to the rim of the shell.

5. Broil approximately 5 minutes or until the edges of the oysters have curled and the topping is bubbling. Watch carefully.

6. Garnish the plates or platter with the parsley sprigs and the lemon wedges. Serve immediately.

Apolline
Boudin
New Orleans, LA

1# Smoked Pork Shoulder
1 cup Chicken Livers
1 each Onion (diced)
3 each Celery Stalk (diced)
¼ Cup Chopped Garlic
1 Tbsp Butter
6 Cups Chicken Stock
3 Cups Aborrio Rice

1 Each Bay Leaf
4 Each Sprigs of Thyme
1 Tbsp Black Pepper
2 Tbsp Salt
1 Tbsp Creole Seasoning
1 Bunch Green Onion
½ Bunch Flat Leaf Parsley

1. Add butter to a sauté pan on medium heat, toss in diced vegetables and cook till translucent.

2. Coarsely chop chicken livers and add to the sauté pan. Cook for 5 min or until livers are cooked

3. Put stock, bay leaf, and thyme in a pot and bring to boil. Add rice and turn to low heat and cover for 20 min or until rice is cooked. Strain off any extra liquid.

4. Shred Pork Shoulder with a fork and add it, along with the rice and vegetable mix, to a bowl and mix until incorporated.

5. Finely chop parsley and green onions and fold it into Boudin mix.

6. Re-season to taste.

7. Stuff rice mix into pork casings and steam for 15-20 min or use rice mix as a stuffing for fish, pork chops, ect...

Established in 1840, Antoine's is the country's oldest family-run restaurant. Jules Alciatore, Antoine's son, invented Oysters Rockefeller, so named for the richness of the sauce. They remain one of the great culinary creations of all time and that recipe remains a closely-guarded Antoine's secret.

Oysters Bienville
Arnaud's
New Orleans, LA

1 Dozen Oysters, shucked and on the halfshell
6 Tbsp Unsalted Butter
1/2 Cup Onion, finely chopped
4 Green Onions, finely sliced
2 Garlic Cloves, minced
6 Tbsp All Purpose Flour
2 Cups Raw Shrimp, peeled and deveined, chopped
1/2 Cup White Mushrooms, finely chopped
1/4 Cup Dry White Wine
1/4 Cup Heavy Cream

Oyster Liquor, reserved
2 Tbsp Italian Parsley, minced
2 Tbsp Fresh Lemon Juice
A few dashes Hot Sauce (I use Crystal)
Kosher Salt, Black Pepper, and Cayenne, to taste
4 Egg Yolks, beaten
Garnish (not meant to be eaten):
1 1/2 Cups Rock Salt
3 Crushed up Bay leaves
1 tsp Whole Cloves
1 tsp Whole Allspice

1. Shuck the oysters, drain off the liquor into a small container; reserve. Leave the oysters on the half shell, refrigerated.

2. Preheat an oven to 400 degrees F.

For the sauce:

1. Melt the butter in a large skillet over medium heat. Add the onions and garlic, saute until the onions turn slightly golden.

2. Add the flour, stirring well to incorporate. Cook for a few minutes until it gets just a bit of color.

3. Stir in the shrimp, mushrooms, and a bit more salt and pepper. Cook for 2-3 minutes, stirring constantly, until the shrimp start to turn pink.

4. Add the white wine and the cream, cook for 2 minutes.

5. Add the lemon juice, parsley, and hot sauce. Season to taste with the salt, pepper, and cayenne; remove from the heat.

6. When the sauce is slightly cooled, stir in the egg yolks, moving quickly to incorporate and keep them from curdling.

For the Oysters:

1. Mix the Rock Salt with remaining garnish ingredients. Heat in the oven in a seperate pie tin at the same time as the oysters.

2. Top each Oyster with about 2 Tbsp of the prepared sauce. Place them in a pan that has a thin layer of rock salt in the bottom, this is to keep the oysters steady.

3. Bake for 10-12 Minutes then turn on the broiler to slightly brown the tops, for 1-2 minutes. The Oysters are finished when the sauce is heated through and the edges of the oysters start to curl.

4. Place the aromatic rock salt mixture on a large plate or platter. Arrange the Oysters Bienville decoratively around the plate. Serve.

Cracklin Crusted Fish and Chips

Bombay Club
New Orleans, LA

For the batter:
2 cups all-purpose flour
1 tablespoon baking powder
1 teaspoon kosher salt 1/4 teaspoon
cayenne pepper
Dash Old Bay Seasoning
1 bottle Miller High Life, cold
1 1/2 pounds flounder or speckled trout,
cut into 1-ounce strips Cornstarch, for
dredging

8 ounces ready puffed cracklings, regular
flavored
** at the restaurant we make shrimp puffs
to serve with our fish and chips. I
recommend serving it with store cut or
fresh cut fries.
For Fresh cut fries:
1 gallon peanut oil
4 large Idaho potatoes
Kosher salt

1. In a bowl, whisk together the flour, baking powder, salt, cayenne pepper, and Old Bay seasoning. Whisk in the beer until the batter is completely smooth and free of any lumps. Refrigerate for 15 minutes. Note: The batter can be made up to 1 hour ahead of time.

2. Place cracklings in a food processer and pulsate 3 to 4 times and set aside for later use

For the frying:

1. Allow the oil to reach 350 degrees. Lightly dredge fish strips in cornstarch. Working in small batches, dip the fish into batter and then coat them with crackling crust. Carefully set into hot oil. When the batter is set, turn the pieces of fish over and cook until golden brown, about 2 minutes. Drain the fish on a roasting rack. Sprinkle with extra Old Bay Seasoning and serve with malt vinegar

For fresh cut fries:

1.Heat the peanut oil in a 5-quart cast iron pot over high heat until it reaches 320 degrees. Using a V-slicer with a wide blade, slice the potatoes with the skin on. Place in a large bowl with cold water.

2. Drain potatoes completely, removing any excess water. When oil reaches 320 degrees, submerge the potatoes in the oil. Working in small batches, fry for 2 to 3 minutes until they are pale and limp. Remove from oil, drain, and cool to room temperature.

3. Increase the temperature of the oil to 375 degrees. Re-immerse fries and cook until crisp and golden brown, about 2 to 3 minutes. Remove and drain on roasting rack. While hot season with kosher salt. Serve immediately

{ *New Orleans was founded in 1718 by Jean Baptiste Le Moyne, Sieur de Bienville. At first, the community was nothing more than a trading camp on the curving east bank of the Mississippi River. Later, the city was organized into a rectangular, fortified community, which still exists today as the French Quarter. The original streets, laid out in a grid, were named for French royalty and nobility.* }

Shrimp with Cheese-Grit Cakes and Bacon Vinaigrette

Boucherie
New Orleans, LA

3 1/2 cups milk
5 garlic cloves, minced
1 cup quick grits
1/2 cup shredded sharp cheddar
Salt and freshly ground pepper
Tabasco
2 tablespoons vegetable oil, plus more for brushing
4 ounces lean bacon, cut into 1/2-inch dice
2 small shallots, minced
1 small celery rib, minced

1 scallion, finely chopped
1/2 red bell pepper, minced
1 tablespoon chopped parsley
1 teaspoon chopped thyme
1/4 cup balsamic vinegar
2 tablespoons Dijon mustard
1 tablespoon Worcestershire sauce
Barbecue spice mix or Cajun seasoning, for dusting
1 pound large shrimp, shelled and deveined

1. Lightly oil a 9-inch-square glass baking dish. In a medium saucepan, bring the milk to a simmer with half of the garlic. Slowly whisk in the grits over moderate heat until very thick, 3 minutes. Remove from the heat and whisk in the cheddar. Season with salt, pepper and Tabasco. Pour into the dish and press plastic wrap directly onto the surface. Let stand until firm, 30 minutes.

2. Meanwhile, in a small skillet, heat the 2 tablespoons of oil. Add the bacon; cook over moderate heat until crisp. Add the shallots, celery, scallion, red pepper, parsley, thyme and the remaining garlic and cook, stirring, until the shallots are softened, about 2 minutes. Off the heat, stir in the vinegar, mustard, Worcestershire and a few dashes of Tabasco. Season with salt and keep warm.

3. Heat a grill pan and brush with oil. Cut the grits into 12 squares and dust on both sides with barbecue spice mix. Cook over moderate heat until crisp, about 2 minutes per side. Keep the grit cakes warm in a low oven; keep the grill pan hot.

4. Brush the shrimp with oil, season with salt and pepper and dust with barbecue spice mix. Grill the shrimp in the pan over moderately high heat until lightly charred and just cooked through, about 1 1/2 minutes per side. Arrange the shrimp and grit cakes on plates, drizzle the bacon vinaigrette on top and serve right away.

Established as the capital of the French colony of Louisiana, New Orleans was actually twice named the state capital. The title of capital city was moved from New Orleans to Donaldsonville in 1825, to Baton Rouge in 1846, to New Orleans in 1864 (during the Reconstruction period), and then again to Baton Rouge in 1879.

Crawfish Pie
Bourbon House
New Orleans, LA

For the Crawfish Filling:
1/2 cup butter
1/4 cup flour
1 cup chopped onion
2 teaspoon garlic, minced
1/3 cup diced bell pepper
3 tablespoons chopped parsley
1 tablespoon chopped celery
1/2 tablespoon minced shallot
1 teaspoon salt
1 teaspoon ground black pepper
dash cayenne pepper

1/8 teaspoon thyme
2 lbs crawfish tail, fat included
1 oz brandy
2 oz heavy cream
For the Pie:
2 1/2 cups sifted flour
1 teaspoon salt
1/2 cup unsalted butter, cut into small pieces
1/2 cup ice water
Louisiana Crawfish Pie

For the Crawfish Filling:

1. In a heavy bottomed Dutch oven, melt butter over medium heat and add flour, cook (stirring constantly) until roux turns golden brown. Add all the vegetables and continue cooking for 5-10 minutes until vegetables are soft. Add brandy and heavy cream and cook over low heat for 10 more minutes. Add salt, black pepper, cayenne, thyme and parsley and fold in crawfish tails. Check for seasoning and cook just until warmed through, approximately 2 minutes.

2. Remove from heat and refrigerate until ready to use.

For the Pie:

1. In a large bowl sift flour and mix in the salt. Add chilled butter and with a pastry cutter, work in the butter until the mixture resembles coarse meal. Add the cold water and mix until dough sticks together. Roll the dough into a ball, wrap and refrigerate. When properly chilled remove the dough and on a lightly floured surface roll out two 1/8th inch circles, one 10 1/2-inch wide and one 12-inches wide. Line a 9 inch pie tin with the larger circle of crust and let the crust hang over the edge. Fill with the prepared filling and place the smaller circle of dough on top. Press and seal the edges and pinch together the edges to form a fluted rim. Cut eight one inch slits radiating from the center of the pie and bake in a preheated 350°F oven for 30 minutes until the crust is golden brown.

Brandy Milk Punch
Brennan's
New Orleans, LA

2 oz. Napoleon brandy
4 oz. half & half
1 oz. simple syrup

¼ oz. vanilla extract
Freshly grated nutmeg for garnish

1. Combine brandy, half & half, simple syrup, and vanilla extract in a cocktail shaker filled with ice. Shake vigorously and pour into a chilled old-fashioned glass. Garnish with nutmeg.

Bananas Foster
Brennan's
New Orleans, LA

1/4 cup (1/2 stick) butter
1 cup brown sugar
1/2 teaspoon cinnamon
1/2 cup banana liqueur

4 bananas, cut in half lengthwise, then halved
1/4 cup dark rum
4 scoops vanilla ice cream

1. Combine the butter, sugar, and cinnamon in a flambé pan or skillet. Place the pan over low heat either on an alcohol burner or on top of the stove, and cook, stirring, until the sugar dissolves. Stir in the banana liqueur, then place the bananas in the pan. When the banana sections soften and begin to brown, carefully add the rum.

2. Continue to cook the sauce until the rum is hot, then tip the pan slightly to ignite the rum. When the flames subside, lift the bananas out of the pan and place four pieces over each portion of ice cream. Generously spoon warm sauce over the top of the ice cream and serve immediately.

Pecan Pie
Brigtsen's
New Orleans, LA

For the dough:
1 cup all purpose flour
1/2 teaspoon salt
7 tablespoons cold unsalted butter
1/4 cup ice water
For the filling:
3 eggs

1 cup granulated white sugar
1 cup dark corn syrup
2 tablespoons melted unsalted butter
1 1/2 teaspoons pure vanilla extract
1/8 teaspoon salt
1/2 cup darkly roasted pecans, ground
1 cup medium pecan pieces

For the dough:

1. Preheat the oven to 350 degrees. Sift the flour and salt into a mixing bowl. Using the large holes of a hand grater, grate the butter into the mixing bowl with the flour mixture. Lightly blend the butter and flour mixture with your fingertips until the texture is like coarse cornmeal. Be careful not to overwork the dough. Add the ice water and blend until thoroughly incorporated. Form the dough into a ball and place it on a floured cutting board. Roll out the dough, adding flour as necessary, to 1/8-inch thick. Place an 8 1/2-inch pie pan face down on the dough and cut the dough to fit the pan, leaving a border of about 1-inch. Line the pie pan with the dough, trim the edges, and refrigerate until ready to use.

For the filling:

1. In an electric mixer with the wire whisk attachment, add the eggs and beat on high speed until frothy, about 1 minute. Add the sugar, corn syrup, butter, vanilla, salt, and ground roasted pecans. Beat on medium speed until well blended. Stir in the pecan pieces. Pour the filling into the pie shell. Bake in a preheated 350 degree oven for 40 minutes. Reduce the heat to 325 degrees and bake until the filling is browned on top and the crust is light golden brown, 35 to 40 minutes. Remove from the oven and cool at room temperature for 1 hour before serving.

Oysters LeRuth
Brigtsen's
New Orleans, LA

2 ½ tbsp. unsalted butter
2 cloves garlic, finely chopped
2 scallions, finely chopped
1 stalk celery, finely chopped
½ small yellow onion, finely chopped
1 tbsp. finely chopped parsley
½ tsp. finely chopped thyme
½ tsp. cayenne pepper
¼ tsp. celery seed
1 bay leaf
Kosher salt and freshly ground white

pepper, to taste
4 oz. raw medium shrimp (about 5), finely chopped
1 tbsp. flour
1 cup heavy cream
2 oz. crabmeat, picked of shells
1 cup fresh bread crumbs
cup grated Parmesan cheese
Coarse rock salt, for pan
12 bluepoint oysters, on the half shell
½ tsp. paprika

1. Melt butter in a 2-qt. saucepan over medium-high heat. Add garlic, scallions, celery, and onions; cook, stirring occasionally, until golden, 4-6 minutes. Add parsley, thyme, cayenne, celery seed, bay, salt, and pepper; cook until fragrant, 1 minute. Add shrimp; cook until just pink; 1-2 minutes. Add flour; cook 1 minute. Add cream and bring to a boil; remove from heat and stir in crab, bread crumbs, and cheese. Transfer to a pastry bag fitted with a ½" fluted tip; refrigerate until cold, at least 1 hour.

2. Heat broiler to high. Line a baking sheet with rock salt about ¼" deep. Nestle oysters onto bed of rock salt. Pipe filling over oysters and sprinkle with paprika; broil until tops are browned, about 4 minutes.

Shrimp Bisque
Broussard's
New Orleans, LA

1/2 carrot, finely chopped
1/2 onion, finely chopped
2 sprigs parsley
1/2 bay leaf
Pinch thyme
1 cup white wine

24 whole raw medium shrimp, washed
3/4 cup flour
2 quarts chicken stock
3 tablespoons cream
2 tablespoons butter
2 tablespoons brandy, sherry, or Madeira

1. In a large saucepan, melt 2 tablespoons butter and add the carrots, onions, parsley, bay leaf, and thyme. Cover the pan and cook the vegetables slowly until they are tender. Add the white wine and the shrimp and poach them for about 8 minutes.

2. Remove and reserve the shrimp.

3. When the shrimp are cool enough to handle, shell and de-vein twelve of them, reserving the shells.

4. Cut the meat into dice and reserve it.

5. Put the shells and the remaining whole shrimp through the food chopper and add the chopped mixture to the kettle with the mirepoix and poaching wine.

6. Stir in the flour. Add the chicken stock, bring the soup back to a boil, and simmer it for 20 minutes.

7. Strain it through a fine sieve and if it is too thick, add a little milk.

8. Strain it again through a thickness of cheesecloth.

9. Just before serving, bring the soup back to a boil and add the cream and 2 tablespoons each of butter and brandy, sherry, or Madeira.

10. Garnish each serving with the reserved diced shrimp.

Stuffed Black-Eyed Pea Fritters
Café Carmo
New Orleans, LA

Fritters:
2 cups dried black-eyed peas
1 medium onion
1 tablespoon salt
1 gallon red palm oil (for frying)
Vatapá (stuffing):
1/2 cup peanuts, ground
1/2 cup cashews, ground
2 medium onions, diced
1 bell pepper, diced
2 tomatoes, diced
1 can coconut milk
2 cups white bread, cubed
1 cup dried shrimp, ground
1/4 cup chopped cilantro, chopped

1 tablespoon extra-virgin organic red palm oil
Salt to taste
Vinaigrette (salsa fresca topping):
1 tomato, chopped
1/4 cup cilantro, chopped
1 medium onion, chopped
1 tablespoon cider vinegar
1/2 teaspoon salt
Shrimp
1 pound fresh 36/40 Gulf shrimp, pealed, deveined and boiled. In the original Brazilian recipe one would use medium reconstituted dried shrimp for topping.

Fritters:

1. Soak black-eyed peas overnight, then drain. Combine all ingredients then emulsify until the mixture becomes homogeneous, the thickness of a soft cookie dough. Place small batches of the batter into a wooden or plastic bowl, and use a wooden spoon to whip (activate) it, for aproximately 10 minutes, or until the mixture doubles in volume. Using a 4" spoon, drop oval-shaped into palm oil and fry until the outside becomes dark brown.

Vatapá (stuffing):

1. Combine bread and coconut milk, set aside. Sauté onions and peppers and tomatoes in a cast iron pan until tomatoes cook apart. Now add the remainder of ingredients and cook on medium for 30-40 minutes, or until the mixture becomes somewhat paste-like.

Plating:

1. Now it's time to put it all together. Split the fritters lengthwise, nearly all the way through. Stuff with a tablespoon or so of vatapá, top with a teaspoon of vinaigrette and a few shrimp. Eat with hot sauce (a vinegar-based brand like Crystal or Trappey's is similar to Brazilian brands)

{ *The largest municipal park in the country, New Orleans' City Park was also home to the famous Duelling Oaks, where Creole gentlemen frequently met to settle scores with swords, pistols, and sometimes even Bowie knives.* }

Beignets
Café du Monde
New Orleans, LA

1 Envelope Active Dry Yeast
3/4 Cup Water (110 degrees F)
1/4 Cup Granulated Sugar
1/2 tsp Salt
1 Beaten Egg

1/2 Cup Evaporated Milk
3 1/2 – 3 3/4 Cups A.P. Flour
1/8 Cup Shortening
Vegetable Oil for Frying
Powdered Sugar in a shaker or sifter

1. Combine the Yeast, Water, and Sugar in the work bowl of a stand mixer fitted with a dough hook. Let this sit until frothy, about 5 minutes, then add the Salt, Egg, and Evaporated Milk. Mix on low speed, then add half of the flour until it starts to come together, then add the shortening. When the shortening is incorporated start adding the remaining flour, a little at a time until most of it is incorporated. At this time I always turn the dough onto a floured bench to finish by hand, just like when I make bread; it's a touch thing. Knead the dough adding just enough flour as necessary to make a non-sticky, smooth dough. Place the dough into a large oiled bowl, loosely cover and let rise (I made mine last night and let it rise overnight in the refrigerator).

2. After the dough has doubled in bulk, punch it down and turn it onto a floured surface and roll out into a rectangle that is about 1/2" thick. With a very sharp knife working at a diagonal to the rectangle, cut into 2" wide strips. Now cut into diamond shapes by making diagonal cuts in the opposite direction. Place the Beignets on a floured baking sheet to let rise about 40 minutes in a warm place.

3. When the Beignets have risen, heat 2-3 inches of vegetable oil in a large saucepan to 350-360 degrees. Place 2-3 Beignets into the hot oil at a time, being careful not to smash or deflate them. When they are golden brown, flip them over until golden brown on the other side. Remove to paper towel lined plates to drain. Serve hot topped with plenty of powdered sugar. Best served with Cafe au Lait.

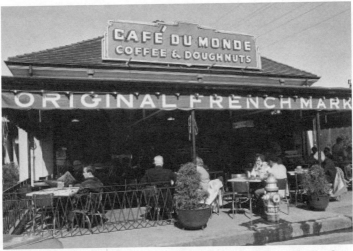

Most people are intrigued when they realize that chicory is actually the root of the endive plant, which is roasted and then ground to be added to the coffee. This is the basis for the famous Cafe au Lait at Cafe du Monde.

New Orleans Muffuletta Sandwich
Central Grocery
New Orleans, LA

1 round loaf Muffuletta Bread or Italian-style bread, 10-inch in diameter
Olive Salad
Extra-virgin olive oil or juice from Olive Salad
2 ounces salami, thinly sliced
2 ounces Italian ham, thinly sliced
2 ounces Provolone cheese, thinly sliced
Muffuletta Olive Salad:
2/3 cup pitted and coarsely-chopped green olives
2/3 cup pitted and coarsely-chopped Kalamata olives
1/2 cup chopped pimiento*
3 cloves garlic, minced
1 anchovy fillet, mashed
1 tablespoon capers, drained and rinsed
1/2 cup finely-chopped fresh parsley leaves
1 teaspoon finely-chopped fresh oregano leaves
1/2 teaspoon freshly-ground pepper
1/2 cup extra-virgin olive oil

1. Either make or purchase your Muffuletta Bread

2. Prepare the Olive Salad.

3. Cut bread in half crosswise (lengthwise) and scoop out about half of the soft dough from top and bottom pieces (this is to provide more room for the sandwich ingredients). Brush the inside bottom of loaf with olive oil or juice from the Olive Salad marinade.

4. Layer salami, Italian ham and Provolone cheese on the bottom piece.

5. Top with as much Olive Salad as will fit without spilling out. Add top of loaf and press down slightly.

6. Slice in quarters and serve. Always serve the prepared Muffuletta Sandwich at room temperature, never toasted.

Muffuletta Olive Salad:

1. In a medium-size bowl, combine all the ingredients and then allow the flavors to mingle for at least 1 hour prior to serving.

2. Store, covered, in the refrigerator until ready to use.

Red Beans and Rice
Chez Helene
6775 Bears Bluff Rd, Wadmalaw Island

1 lb red beans
1 lb Smoked ham hock
1 onion, chopped
1/2 green bell pepper, chopped
salt and pepper and Creole seasoning to taste
2 cloves garlic
1/2 stick butter

1. Pick through beans and remove any rocks. Wash beans and cover with water by a good three inches. Let soak overnight (adding more water to keep the beans covered), rinse, change the water and add onion, bell pepper, ham hock and garlic.

2. Cook on slow fire, in a heavy bottomed 6 qt. pot until done (about 2 hours). Add salt, pepper, and butter and cook 5 minutes.

3. Serve over rice with Louisiana hot sauce, French bread and butter.

Crab Cakes
Clementine's Restaurant
New Orleans, LA

1/2 cup diced celery
1/2 cup diced red bell pepper
1 tablespoon chopped garlic
1 stick unsalted butter
1 cup diced onions
2 tablespoons crab base
1 cup white wine
1 quart heavy cream
Blonde roux

1/2 cup chopped parsley
3/4 cup chopped green onions
2 lbs lump crabmeat
1/2 cup Parmesan cheese
Flour
Panko bread crumbs
Eggwash
Oil for frying

1. Sauté the first five ingredients in a skillet on medium heat until vegetables become translucent and soft, 8-10 minutes. Add Crab Base and White Wine. Cook over Medium-High Heat until White Wine has reduced by half, 6-10 minutes. Add Cream and bring to a boil. Add Blonde roux to thicken. Mixture works best when it is a heavy dip consistency.

2. Add seasonings to taste. Add parsley and green onions. Pour mixture onto a sheet pan and allow to cool in refrigerator for 1 hour.

3. Once cool, fold in crabmeat and parmesan cheese. Portion to desired size. Dredge each Crabcake into flour, eggwash, then Panko breadcrumbs. Deep fry or fry in a skillet for 3 minutes on each side at 300°F, until golden. Garnish with a lemon twist & Chive, serve hot.

Calas with Apple, Currant and Celery Salad
Cochon
New Orleans, LA

¼ cup dried currants
Approx. ½ cup canola or grapeseed oil
1 small onion, diced (about ¾ cups)
1 tablespoon minced garlic
2 cups cooked rice, long or mediumgrain
6 small green onions, white and light-green parts only, sliced thin crosswise (about 5 tablespoons)
½ cup flour
2 teaspoons baking powder

Salt and pepper
1 egg, lightly beaten
¾ cup buttermilk or milk
2 tart green apples
3 small celery stalks, sliced thin crosswise (about 1 cup)
1 bunch watercress
1 teaspoon prepared horseradish, to taste
2 tablespoons red wine vinegar
4 tablespoons extra-virgin olive oil

1. Bring water kettle to boil. Place currants in small bowl and pour over enough water to just cover. Set aside.

2. Set medium sauté pan over medium heat. Swirl in 1 tablespoon canola or grapeseed oil. Add onion and garlic. Stirring frequently, cook 2-3 minutes, or until onion is translucent and garlic is golden. Remove from heat.

3. In large bowl, combine rice, green onions, flour, baking powder and 1 teaspoon salt, stirring until clump-free. Mix in egg and milk. Add onions and garlic and stir. Season with salt and pepper.

4. Set large skillet, with enough canola or grapeseed oil to coat bottom of pan with ¼ inch oil, over medium heat. Once a droplet of water sizzles but doesn't spurt when it hits the oil, spoon in 3-4 calas, about ¼ cup batter for each. Do not overcrowd pan.

5. Fry calas 3 minutes, or until golden and crisp at edges. Flip and fry 2 minutes, or until golden. Transfer calas to a cooling rack set over a sheet tray. Sprinkle with salt. Repeat until all batter is used, adding extra oil to pan and adjusting heat as needed.

6. While calas fry, halve, core and slice apples into thin half-moons. Strain plumped currants and pat dry. In large bowl, toss apple, celery and currants. Add watercress and toss to combine.

7. In small bowl, stir horseradish and vinegar together. Whisk in olive oil. Season with salt and pepper to taste. Toss salad with dressing. Adjust seasoning.

8. To serve, place two calas on each plate with salad alongside.

Catfish Courtbouillon
Cochon
New Orleans, LA

2 red bell peppers
2 green bell peppers
2 poblano peppers
1 jalapeño pepper
3 medium tomatoes
1 whole head garlic
5 tablespoons vegetable oil, divided
2 tablespoons butter
1 large onion, diced (about 1 cup)
6 medium cloves garlic, chopped (about 1/4 cup)
2 cups fish or seafood stock (for testing purposes, we used Kitchen Basics brand)
1/2 cup red wine vinegar
Hot sauce, to taste
Salt, to taste
Freshly ground pepper, to taste
1/4 cup fresh mint leaves
1/4 cup fresh parsley
4 green onions, sliced
1/2 teaspoon lemon juice
1 cup all-purpose flour
1 cup self-rising white cornmeal mix
2 pounds small catfish fillets
Hot cooked rice

1. Preheat broiler. Broil peppers and tomatoes on a foil-lined baking sheet 5 inches from heat, with oven door partially open, about 5 minutes on each side or until blistered. Place in a heavy-duty zip-top plastic bag; seal and let stand 10 minutes to loosen skins. Open bag, and allow to cool. Peel peppers and tomatoes; remove and discard seeds and stems from peppers.

2. Reduce oven temperature to 400°. Cut off pointed end of garlic head; place on a piece of aluminum foil, and drizzle with 1 tablespoon oil. Fold foil to seal. Bake at 1 hour; remove and allow to cool. Squeeze pulp from garlic cloves, and place in a food processor with peeled peppers and tomatoes. Pulse until roughly chopped and a chunky consistency.

3. Melt butter in a large saucepan over medium heat. Add onion, and cook until soft and just beginning to brown, about 8 minutes. Add chopped raw garlic, and cook 1 minute more. Stir in chopped pepper mixture.

4. Add stock and vinegar, and bring to a low boil. Simmer, uncovered, 30 minutes or until sauce has a thick, stew-like consistency. Season with hot sauce, salt, and pepper. Stir in mint and next 3 ingredients.

5. Combine flour and cornmeal in a shallow dish. Season catfish with salt and pepper, and dredge in cornmeal mixture, pressing to adhere. Heat remaining 4 tablespoons oil in a large skillet over high heat, and fry catfish in batches, 3 minutes per side or until cooked through. Transfer to a paper towel-lined baking sheet, and place in a 200° oven to keep warm.

6. Place rice on a large serving platter. Remove fish from oven, and arrange on top of rice. Spoon sauce over fish and serve remaining sauce alongside. Season with salt, pepper, and hot sauce to taste.

Smoked Goose and Foie Gras Gumbo
Commander's Palace
New Orleans, LA

1 cup rendered goose fat
1 cup flour
5 cloves garlic, minced
3 stalks celery, minced
1 green bell pepper, minced
1 large yellow onion, minced
1 lb. white button mushrooms, minced
2 tsp. kosher salt, plus more to taste
1 tsp. Creole seasoning
½ tsp. freshly ground black pepper
2 bay leaves

10 cups chicken stock
12 oz. smoked goose, roughly chopped
1 lb. chanterelle, porcini, or oyster
mushrooms, cut into 1" pieces
1 tsp. hot sauce
1 tsp. Worcestershire sauce
½ tsp. minced thyme
3 oz. foie gras, puréed
Sliced scallions, for garnish
Cooked white rice, for serving

1. Melt goose fat in an 8-qt. Dutch oven over high. Sprinkle in flour; whisk until smooth. Reduce heat to medium-low; cook, whisking constantly, until roux is the color of peanut butter, 25–30 minutes. Add garlic, celery, bell pepper, and onion; cook until soft, 10–12 minutes. Add button mushrooms, salt, Creole seasoning, black pepper, and bay leaves; cook 2 minutes. Whisk in stock; boil. Reduce heat to medium; cook, skimming fat as needed, until thickened, about 1 hour. Add smoked goose, chanterelles, hot and Worcestershire sauces, thyme, and salt; cook until goose is warmed through and mushrooms are tender, 12–15 minutes. Ladle into bowls; garnish with puréed foie gras and scallions. Serve with rice.

Steen's Marinated Pork Tenderloin
Criollo
New Orleans, LA

1/4 cup walnut oil
2 tablespoons minced ginger
3/4 cup Steen's cane molasses
1 large red onion, diced

1 teaspoon kosher salt
1 teaspoon black pepper
6 7-ounce pieces pork tenderloin
2 tabelspoons olive oil

1. In a large, non-reactive bowl, thoroughly combine the walnut oil, ginger, molasses, onion, salt, and pepper; add the pork pieces and turn to coat evenly. Marinate, turning pork occasionally, at least 12 hours or overnight.

2. Preheat oven to 350°F.

3. Bring pork to room temperature. Heat oil in a large cast iron skillet over medium-high heat. Add pork and sear on all sides. Transfer skillet to oven and roast pork to desired doneness, 140°F recommended (10-15 minutes, depending on thickness). Let rest 8 minutes, slice each serving piece into 3-4 thin slices and serve at once.

Pan-Seared Prime Beef With Louisiana Crawfish Ragout
Dickie Brennan's Steakhouse
New Orleans, LA

4 prime beef medallions (about 4 ounces each)
kosher salt and cracked black pepper
1 tablespoon chopped fresh garlic
1/4 cup olive oil
1/2 cup chopped white onion
1 red bell pepper, chopped
1/2 cup chicken stock
1/2 pound Louisiana crawfish tails
2 tablespoons fresh thyme
1/2 cup (1 stick) butter, chilled and chopped
1 bunch green onions, finely chopped
creole seasoning

1. Preheat a large skillet (nonstick or coated with a tablespoon of oil) over high heat. Season beef on all sides with salt and pepper. Sear beef on each side for about a minute, then move to a platter and keep warm.

2. Using the same skillet, toast garlic in olive oil. Add onion and red bell pepper and sauté until onion is translucent. Add stock and stir well with a wooden spoon, scraping the bottom of the skillet to deglaze. Cook until the liquid reduces by half. Add crawfish tails and thyme. Add butter a few pieces at a time, whisking to incorporate after each addition. Fold in green onions. Season to taste with salt, pepper, and Creole seasoning.

3. To serve, spoon crawfish ragout over beef medallions.

The monument to General Andrew Jackson at Jackson Square was the world's first equestrian statue in which the horse had more than one foot off the base.

Sweet Potato Pie
Dooky Chase
New Orleans, LA

Crust:

1 1/2 cups unbleached all-purpose flour

1 teaspoon salt

1/4 cup finely-chopped pecans

1/2 cup cold butter (the original recipe calls for vegetable shortening)

1/4 cups ice-cold water, or as needed

Filling:

2 large sweet potatoes (about 1.5 lbs total), peeled and cut into 2-inch cubes

1/2 cup sugar

1 teaspoon ground cinnamon

1/4 teaspoon ground nutmeg

2 large eggs, slightly beaten

1/4 cup condensed milk

1/2 teaspoon vanilla extract

1 tablespoon melted butter

Pecan halves for decoration

Crust:

In a food processor, pulse together all the dry ingredients and the butter into short bursts until the mixture forms pea-sized lumps. Add the water through the feed chute as you pulse until the mixture forms a stiff dough and pulls away from the sides of the food processor bowl. Form the dough into a 6-inch disk and wrap it in plastic; chill for one hour. The dough can be made in advance. It can be kept refrigerated for several days and even frozen.

Methods:

1. Preheat the oven to 375 degrees F.

2. Roll the chilled pie dough into a 12-inch round and press into a 9-inch pie pan. Flute the edges. Bake for 10-15 minutes until the crust is set and beginning to brown slightly. Remove the pie pan from the oven and let it cool.

3. Put the sweet potatoes into a medium pot and cover them with water by an inch. Bring to a boil. Boil slowly until the potatoes are tender with no absolutely no resistance at the center when pieced with a fork.

4. Drain off the water and mash the potatoes with a potato masher. Do not use a potato ricer or food processor.

5. As you mash the potatoes, add the sugar, cinnamon, and nutmeg; then whisk in the eggs, milk, and vanilla. The butter goes in last.

6. Once the filling is well-mixed, pour it into the baked pie crust. Arrange pecan halves around the outside edges and sprinkle the top of the pie with more ground cinnamon. Bake for 20-25 minutes until the filling is set and the edges of the crust have browned.

7. Serve the pie warm or at room temperature with whipped cream or vanilla ice cream.

When ice got too expensive, some Creole families who loved to entertain would crush glass and sew it into cheesecloth bags, floating the bags in water pitchers to mimic the tinkle of ice.

Charbroiled Oysters
Drago's Seafood Restaurant
New Orleans, LA

ᴋs (2 sticks) softened butter
ᴊlespoons finely chopped garlic
1 teaspoon black pepper
Pinch dried oregano
1 1/2 dozen large, freshly shucked oysters

on the half shell
1/4 cup grated Parmesan and Romano
cheeses, mixed
2 teaspoons chopped flat-leaf parsley

Note: Tommy Cvitanovich of Drago's Seafood Restaurant says, "This is the perfect dish for those who want to enjoy oysters in their unadorned form, but can't or won't eat them raw. Once you start eating these charbroiled ones, you won't be able to stop. Don't attempt this without freshly shucked oysters and an outdoor grill."

1. Heat a gas or charcoal grill. In a medium bowl, mix butter with garlic, pepper, and oregano.

2. Place oysters on the half shell right over the hottest part. Spoon enough of the seasoned butter over the oysters so that some of it will overflow into the fire and flame up a bit.

3. The oysters are ready when they puff up and get curly on the sides, about 5 minutes. Sprinkle the grated Parmesan and Romano and the parsley on top. Serve on the shells immediately with hot French bread.

Creole Potato Salad
Dunbar's Restaurant
New Orleans, LA

5 pounds Irish potatoes
6 hard-boiled eggs, chopped
3 generous tablespoons sweet pickle relish
1 generous tablespoon yellow mustard
1 teaspoon black pepper (or to taste)

1 tablespoon Creole seasoning-spice mix (or to taste)
2 tablespoons dried parsley
1/2 cup mayonnaise
Optional garnish: Sliced hard-boiled egg.
Sprigs of fresh curly parsley

1. Peel and coarsely dice potatoes. Cook in boiling water until tender, about 20 minutes. Drain.

2. In large bowl combine potatoes and remaining ingredients. Gently fold to incorporate. Allow to cool.

3. Garnish with sliced egg and parsley.

4. Maybe be served at room temperature or chilled.

In 1813, Governor Claiborne offered a $500 reward for the capture of legendary pirate Jean Lafitte; Lafitte countered by posting a $1,500 reward for the capture of Claiborne.

Coconut Cream Pie
Emeril's Delmonico
New Orleans, LA

1 recipe Cashew Pie Crust, blind baked and cooled, (recipe follows)
2½ cups milk
¾ cup sugar
4 eggs, whisked
¼ cup cornstarch
½ stick unsalted butter, at room temperature
1 teaspoon coconut extract, or to taste*
1 recipe Lime Meringue, (recipe follows), or whipped cream
Cashew Pie Crust
1 stick unsalted butter
1¼ cup all purpose flour

¼ cup cashews, ground
Pinch of salt
Pinch of lime zest
1 teaspoon vanilla extract
1 egg yolk
Lime Meringue
For the syrup:
1 cup plus 2 tablespoons sugar
¼ cup water
¼ cup freshly squeezed lime juice
For the whites:
3 large egg whites
1 tablespoon plus 1 teaspoon sugar
Zest of 2 limes

1. Place milk and sugar in a heavy saucepan and bring just to a boil, stirring until sugar is dissolved.

2. In a medium bowl, whisk together the eggs and cornstarch until smooth. Whisk about a cup of the hot milk mixture into the eggs to temper, then add the egg-milk mixture back to the pot. Reduce the temperature to medium-low and continue to cook, whisking constantly, until mixture is very thick and any starchy taste is gone, 5 to 10 minutes.

3. Remove from heat and whisk in the butter and coconut extract, then immediately strain the custard through a very fine strainer into a bowl. Set the bowl inside a larger bowl that is filled with an ice bath and stir occasionally until the custard has cooled slightly. Transfer the custard to the cooled pie shell and refrigerate, covered with plastic wrap, until thoroughly chilled. When the custard is firm and pie is completely cooled, top the pie with the Lime Meringue or, if preferred, with whipped cream.

Cashew Pie Crust:

1. Cut the butter into small pieces and place in the freezer until very well-chilled.

2. Place flour, cashews, salt, and lime zest in a food processor. Add the chilled butter and pulse the processor until the butter is the size of small peas. Add the egg yolk and vanilla extract and pulse until dough just begins to come together. You may need to add a bit of ice water, a teaspoon at a time, depending on the size of your egg yolk. Gather the dough into a flattened disc, wrap in plastic wrap, and refrigerate for at least 1 hour and up to overnight.

3. On a lightly floured surface and using a floured rolling pin, roll the dough out to a thickness of about 1/8-inch and carefully place in pie dish. Trim the excess dough to about ½-inch and tuck edges into sides of pie dish. Crimp the edges decoratively and refrigerate the pie crust for 1 hour.

4. Preheat the oven to 400°F and dock the pie crust all over using the tines of a fork. Line the pie crust with parchment paper and fill with pie weights. Bake the pie shell in oven until the sides are set, 8 to 12 minutes, then remove the parchment and pie weights and continue to cook until the crust is golden brown and flakey, 8 to 10 minutes longer. Set crust aside to cool on a wire rack.

Lime Meringue:

1. For the syrup, place the sugar, water, and lime juice in a heavy bottomed sauce pan and cook over high heat until the mixture reaches between 230°F and 240°F on a candy thermometer, about 4 to 5 minutes. Remove from the heat.

2. While the sugar-lime mixture is cooking, place the egg whites and the 1 tablespoon plus 1 teaspoon sugar in the bowl of an electric mixer fitted with the whisk attachment and beat on high speed until the egg whites hold soft peaks.

3. Slowly drizzle the hot syrup into the egg whites while continuing to beat on high speed, until the meringue cools to lukewarm, about 5 minutes. Fold in the lime zest. Spread the meringue over the top of the cooled coconut pie.

Cajun Seafood Rice Casserole
Falcon Rice Mills
New Orleans, LA

2 cups cooked Cajun Country Medium Grain Rice
5 tablespoons butter, divided
1 8-ounce package cream cheese
1 medium onion, chopped
1 bell pepper, chopped
2 cloves garlic, minced
3 oz. fresh mushrooms, roughly chopped

1 lb peeled and deveined Louisiana shrimp
1 lb fresh Louisiana crabmeat
3/4 teaspoon salt
1/4 teaspoon cayenne pepper
1/4 teaspoon black pepper
1/2 cup Ritz cracker crumbs

1. Preheat oven to 350°F.

2. In a small saucepan, melt cream cheese and 1/2 stick butter together on low heat.

3. In a separate saucepan add remaining 1/2 stick butter, onion, bell pepper, garlic and mushrooms. Sauté until vegetables are tender. Add shrimp, salt, cayenne pepper and black pepper. Sauté until shrimp are pink. Add rice and cream cheese mixture; mix well. Gently spoon in crabmeat. Pour into a 3 quart casserole dish. Sprinkle with cracker crumbs. Bake until golden and bubbly, about 30 minutes. Serve hot.

Pimiento Cheese Spread
Fulton Alley
New Orleans, LA

1 cup shredded gruyere
1/2 cup shredded cheddar
6 ounces softened cream cheese
1/4 cup aioli*
1/4 teaspoon garlic powder
1/4 teaspoon cayenne
1/4 teaspoon onion powder
1 teaspoon diced jalapeño
1 teaspoon diced anaheim pepper
2 teaspoon diced roasted red pepper

Aioli:
4 cloves garlic, minced
2 egg yolks
1 cup extra virgin olive oil
2 teaspoons lemon juice
salt to tast
ground black pepper to taste

1. Combine all ingredients and mix thoroughly (serve with toast points or crackers).

Aioli:

1. In a medium bowl, beat eggs well with a wire whisk. Stir in garlic. Gradually add oil in a thin stream, beating constantly until light and creamy.

2. Season with salt and pepper. Stir in lemon juice.

Crabmeat Sardou
Galatoire's
New Orleans, LA

2 tbsp. plus 1 tsp. fresh lemon juice
12 fresh or frozen cleaned, trimmed, and stemmed artichoke hearts
2 lbs. fresh spinach, stemmed
5 tbsp. unsalted butter, cubed and chilled
1 small yellow onion, finely chopped
2 tbsp. flour
1 cup milk

¼ cup heavy cream
Kosher salt and freshly ground white pepper, to taste
6 egg yolks
2 tsp. red wine vinegar
Cayenne pepper, to taste
2 ½ cups clarified butter
2 lbs. jumbo lump crabmeat

1. Bring a large pot of water to a boil and add 2 tbsp. lemon juice and artichoke hearts; cook, stirring occasionally, until just tender, about 12 minutes. Using a slotted spoon, transfer artichoke hearts to a bowl; cover with aluminum foil, set aside, and keep warm.

2. Cream the spinach: Return pot of water to a boil and add spinach; cook, stirring occasionally, until spinach is tender, 3–4 minutes. Drain spinach and transfer to the center of a tea towel. Fold up the edges of the towel and squeeze to expel as much liquid as possible. Transfer spinach to a cutting board, roughly chop, and set aside. Heat 3 tbsp. butter in a 4-qt. saucepan over medium heat and add onions; cook, stirring often, until soft, 4–5 minutes. Whisk in flour and cook for 1 minute. Add milk and bring to a boil; cook, stirring, until thickened, 1 minute. Stir in reserved spinach and cream and cook until hot, 3–4 minutes. Remove pan from heat and season with salt and pepper; set aside and keep warm.

3. Make hollandaise: Combine remaining lemon juice, butter, egg yolks, vinegar, and cayenne in a medium bowl set over a pan of simmering water; cook, whisking constantly, until sauce triples in volume, about 5 minutes. Meanwhile, heat 2 cups clarified butter in a small saucepan over medium heat. Whisking constantly, slowly drizzle warmed clarified butter in a thin stream into yolk mixture until sauce is smooth; set aside and keep warm.

4. To serve, heat remaining clarified butter in a 10" skillet over medium heat and add crabmeat; cook, stirring gently, until crabmeat is heated through, about 3 minutes. Remove from heat. Divide creamed spinach between 6 serving plates and top each with 2 artichoke hearts. Top each artichoke with some of the crab mixture and a generous spoonful of hollandaise. Serve immediately.

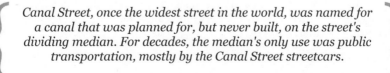

Canal Street, once the widest street in the world, was named for a canal that was planned for, but never built, on the street's dividing median. For decades, the median's only use was public transportation, mostly by the Canal Street streetcars.

Dirty Rice
Herbsaint
New Orleans, LA

1/2 cup chicken livers (8 to 10 medium livers)
2 tablespoons canola oil
1/4 pound ground pork
1 1/2 teaspoons salt
1/2 teaspoon ground pepper
1/2 teaspoon chili powder
1 1/2 cups chicken stock, divided

1 small onion, finely chopped (about 3/4 cup)
2 stalks celery, finely chopped (about 1/2 cup)
2 garlic cloves, minced
1 jalapeño pepper, finely chopped
3 green onions, chopped (about 1/3 cup)
2 tablespoons chopped fresh parsley
3 cups cooked rice

1. Puree chicken livers in a food processor. Heat oil in a large skillet over high heat; add liver and pork, and cook, stirring, until browned, about 4 minutes. Stir in salt, pepper, and chili powder, and cook 2 minutes more.

2. Add 1/4 cup stock, and cook until evaporated, about 8 minutes, allowing mixture to brown and stick to skillet. Stir in onion and next 3 ingredients, and cook until well browned and sticking to skillet, about 8 minutes.

3. Add remaining 1 1/4 cups stock, and cook 2 minutes, stirring to loosen particles from bottom of skillet. Add green onion, parsley, and rice, remove from heat, and stir thoroughly.

Chile-roasted Shrimp
Herbsaint
New Orleans, LA

1/4 cup plus 2 tablespoons olive oil, divided
1 pound large fresh shrimp, unpeeled
3 green jalapeño peppers, stemmed (not seeded) and thinly sliced
1 tablespoon salt

1 tablespoon dried oregano
1 teaspoon ground pepper
Juice of 1 lemon (about 3 tablespoons)
2 garlic cloves, thinly sliced
3/4 cup shrimp stock or water
1 tablespoon butter

1. Combine 1/4 cup olive oil and next 7 ingredients in a large bowl, and toss well. Cover with plastic wrap, and chill at least 2 hours or up to 6 hours.

2. Preheat oven to 450°. Place a 15- x 10-inch jellyroll pan in oven 10 minutes or until extremely hot. Carefully spread shrimp in a single layer across pan. Bake 8 minutes, stirring once halfway through cooking.

3. Remove from oven, and immediately add stock or water, butter, and remaining 2 tablespoons olive oil to pan. Stir well. Serve in shallow bowls with good bread and cold beer or dry German Riesling.

Baked Gulf Oysters with Country Ham, Braised Greens and Cornbread Crumbs
High Hat Café
New Orleans, LA

2 tablespoons olive oil mixed with 2 tablespoons melted butter

1/2 stick (4 tablespoons) butter plus 12 thin pats butter

4 slices country ham, soaked overnight, coarsely chopped

2 onions, finely chopped

2 cloves garlic, sliced

2 bunches mustard greens, cut in a fine julienne

salt and freshly ground black pepper to taste

2 cups cornbread crumbs

12 Gulf oysters, shucked, on the half shell

1. Preheat oven to 350°F.

2. Add butter and olive oil mixture to a very large, heavy pan set over medium-high heat.

3. Add ham, onions, and garlic and cook until soft.

4. Add greens and cook for 20 minutes or until wilted. Season with salt and pepper.

5. Strain greens to remove excess liquid. Cool.

6. Add cornbread crumbs and mix thoroughly.

7. Divide the stuffing evenly atop the oysters in their shells.

8. Top each with a thin pat of butter.

9. Bake for 10 to 15 minutes until bubbly and golden.

Baked Macaroni and Cheese
Jack Dempsey's
New Orleans, LA

1 package macaroni

1 8-ounce Philadelphia cream cheese

1 can evaporated milk

1 stick butter or margarine

1 can Campbell's cheddar cheese soup

2 eggs, beaten

1 8-ounce package shredded sharp cheddar cheese

1. Boil macaroni according to package directions. While macaroni is boiling, take a 9x13 inch pan and place it over the boiling water. Add to the pan (to soften) the cream cheese, butter, and cheese soup. When softened, add the evaporated milk and eggs and mix well.

2. When the macaroni is done, drain and add it to the ingredients in the pan and mix well. Add shredded cheese. Bake in 350 degree oven for 25-30 minutes.

The game of craps was brought in New Orleans by Bernard de Marigny; its name probably derives from "crapaud," the French word for "frog," since some Americans thought of the French as frog-eaters.

Alligator, Sausage and Shrimp Cheesecake

Jacques-Imo's Cafe's
New Orleans, LA

1/3 cup bread crumbs
1 cup Parmesan cheese
4 oz butter, melted
1¾ lb cream cheese, softened
4 eggs
2/3 cup cream
1 cup smoked Gouda cheese, grated
1 cup onion, medium diced
½ cup green pepper, medium diced

½ cup yellow bell pepper, diced
½ cup red bell pepper, diced
1 lb alligator sausage, diced
¼ cup green chili pepper, diced
1 lb shrimp, diced (2 cups)
2 tspn salt
1 tspn chipotle powder
½ tspn black pepper
½ tspn white pepper

1. Mix bread crumbs and cheese; add butter and press into a 10" springform pan.

2. Bake 10 minutes in a 400°F oven to set crust.

3. Whisk the cream cheese until smooth; add eggs and whisk; then add cream and the Gouda cheese.

4. Sauté veggies with spices until soft. Add shrimp and cook until just done.

5. Add sausage and chili pepper, and fold into cream cheese mixture. Wrap foil around pan to prevent leakage and fill pan with mix.

6. Bake in water bath in a 350°F oven for 1½ to 2 hours.

7. Remove when an inserted knife comes out clean and the filling is set.

8. Cool before cutting. Remove from spring mold, cut into 12 pieces

New Orleans, late 1890. Mule drawn tram at Henry Clay Monument, Canal Street & St. Charles.

Fried Oysters, Grilled Slab of Tasso & Saffron Cream
Kingfish
New Orleans, LA

Grilled slab of Tasso Ham
2 3oz. slices of Tasso (Cajun ham)
Non-stick oil spray
Saffron cream
2 tsp. Worcestershire sauce
1 tsp. Dijon mustard
1 shallot, diced
Rounded 1/4 teaspoon crumbled saffron threads
3 Tbsp. olive oil

1 cup dry white wine
1 cup heavy cream
Fried Oysters
½ cup all-purpose flour, divided
½ cup cornmeal
½ cup corn flour
3 tsp. seafood seasoning
6 oysters, shucked
2 cups vegetable oil

Grilled slab of Tasso Ham

Spray tasso with non-stick oil and place on hot grill until grill marks appear. Remove and use in preparation of saffron cream.

Saffron cream

Cook shallot with saffron and in oil in a wide 6- to 8-quart heavy pot (covered) over moderately high heat, stirring occasionally until shallot is softened--about 5 minutes.

Add wine and bring to a boil, then stir in cream, Dijon mustard and Worcesterhire sauce. Add grilled tasso and cook, covered, checking after about 4 minutes until thickened enough to coat the back of a spoon.

Fried Oysters

Combine 1/4 cup all-purpose flour, cornmeal, and 2 teaspoons seafood seasoning in a shallow bowl or pan.

Sprinkle remaining seafood seasoning on oysters and dredge oysters in cornmeal mixture.

Pour oil to a depth of 1/4 to 1/2 inch in a large cast-iron skillet; heat to 385°. Drop oysters into hot oil, and cook about 1 minute or until golden. Drain on paper towels or a rack.

Assembly

Place Saffron Cream with Tasso Ham in a deep serving dish and top the Tasso Ham with fried oysters. Sprinkle with parsley and enjoy with prepared garlic bread.

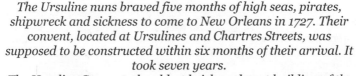

The Ursuline nuns braved five months of high seas, pirates, shipwreck and sickness to come to New Orleans in 1727. Their convent, located at Ursulines and Chartres Streets, was supposed to be constructed within six months of their arrival. It took seven years.
The Ursuline Convent, the oldest brick-and-post building of the French Colonial style in America, also housed the nation's first girls' school.

Blue Crab and Summer Vegetable Soup
Le Petite Grocery
New Orleans, LA

1/2 pound blue crab bodies, rinsed and dried
4 tablespoons vegetable oil
1 cup tomatoes, coarsely chopped
1 carrot, peeled and medium diced
2 large yellow onions, medium diced
2 celery stalks, medium diced
2 whole bay leaves
15 whole black peppercorns
1 ounce fresh thyme, tied with twine
Vegetables:
1 quart prepared crab broth (from preceding recipe)

3 ounces seasonal greens, chopped small
1 tablespoon vegetable oil
1/2 cup mirlitons, small dice
1/2 cup sweet red bell pepper, peeled and diced small
2 cups ripe heirloom tomatoes, concassé
1/2 pound Louisiana jumbo lump crabmeat, picked for shells
salt, to taste
white pepper, to taste
extra-virgin olive oil, to taste
1/2 cup fresh herbs, picked and left whole
Blue Crab and Summer Vegetable Soup

1. Break up the crab bodies and set aside. Heat oil in a 12-quart stock pot. Once oil is nice and hot, add crab bodies one by one, being sure not to splash oil on your arms. Stir with a large spoon over high heat until all the water is cooked out of the crabs and they begin to turn dark red and/or golden in color. As bits of crab begin to stick to the bottom of the pot, scrape them off with your spoon: This is called "fond" and adds lots of flavor. Once your crabs are dry and you have developed plenty of fond, add your tomatoes, carrots, onion, and celery. Stir to incorporate and cover with water 3 inches above the crabs and vegetables. Add herbs and spices. Bring to a boil and turn down to medium-low heat. Let simmer for 1 1/2 hours. Strain through a chinoise three times and chill. Hold under refrigeration until needed.

Vegetable to complete

2. Heat broth to a simmer. In the pot with the broth, add the greens and let simmer about 5 minutes. Meanwhile in a medium sauté pan, heat 1 tablespoon of vegetable oil and sauté the mirlitons for 1 minute. Add red peppers and continue to sauté for 30 more seconds. In 5 soup bowls, divide the heirloom tomato, mirliton, red bell pepper, and jumbo crab. Season broth to taste with salt and white pepper. Pour over veggies in bowls and garnish with lots of fresh herbs and olive oil.

Crawfish Bisque Le Meritage
Le Meritage, Maison Dupuy Hotel
New Orleans, LA

1 tablespoon olive oil
4 tablespoons butter
2 pounds cooked crawfish tails, pre-seasoned
4 medium white onions, diced
5 large baking potatoes, cut into

bite-sized pieces
1 pint heavy cream
chives, chopped, for garnish salt, to taste
pepper, to taste
2 ounces cognac
shrimp stock

1. In a large stock pot, combine the butter and oil, cook until hot. Add the onion and crawfish. Sauté for 20 minutes. Add the cut potatoes and shrimp stock and cook over medium low heat for 1 hour.

2. Puree the soup in a blender. Add 1 pint of heavy cream and the cognac, stir. Salt and pepper the soup to taste.

3. Pour into soup bowls and garnish with the other pound of tails and chives.

4. Serve hot.

Country-Style Meat Pies
Le Petite Grocery
New Orleans, LA

1/4 cup Louisiana popcorn rice

1 pound pork shoulder, cut into 1-inch cubes

4 tablespoons vegetable oil

1/4 pound duck livers, cleaned of veins and fat

1 onion, small dice

5 cloves of garlic, minced

1 teaspoon cayenne pepper

1 tablespoon fresh sage, chopped

1 tablespoon fresh thyme, chopped

1/4 cup fresh parsley, chopped

1/4 cup fresh chives, snipped

1 bunch green onion, finely sliced

kosher salt, to taste

black pepper, to taste

Dough

4 cups all purpose flour

2 teaspoons salt

1 teaspoon baking powder

1/2 cup shortening

2 eggs

1 cup milk

Filling

1. Place 1/2 cup of water and popcorn rice in a medium pot. Bring to a boil, then turn to low and cover.

2. Let cook 15 minutes. Set aside to cool.

3. Sear pork in a medium stock pot over high heat. Once it starts to get color, add just enough water to come halfway up the pork. Bring to a boil then turn down the heat and simmer 2 hours or until completely tender and cuts with a spoon.

4. Drain and reserve meat [shredded]and liquid.

5. Dry duck livers with paper towels and season with salt and black pepper. In a large skillet heat oil until very hot and sear duck livers just until medium rare. Remove the duck livers with a slotted spoon and place in the refrigerator to cool.

6. In the same pan add the onions and garlic and sauté until they start to turn golden brown. Add cooked pork. Using a spoon, work the pork together with onions and garlic (this takes some elbow grease) until mixture is almost paste-like.

7. Add the reserved cooking liquid from the pork and stir to combine. Add the rice.

8. At this point the mixture should resemble stew. Add water to thin it out. Chop the cold duck livers and add them to the pork and rice mixture. Cook mixture at an aggressive simmer for 2 hours. You have to keep an eye on this and add water as needed so it does not burn. The final product should be thick and paste-like. Add all of the fresh herbs and cayenne. Season to taste with salt and pepper and chill until needed.

Dough

1. Combine the flour, salt and baking powder in a large mixing bowl. Cut in the shortening with a pastry blender or 2 large forks. Combine the eggs, and milk in a separate bowl then gently combine all to form a dough. Let rest in cooler for 1 hour before rolling out for meat pies.

2. Dough can hold for up to 5 days.

To assemble the pies

1. You'll need the filling, dough, and 1 cup of egg wash. Roll out the chilled dough to 1/4-inch thickness on a floured surface. Cut into circles using a biscuit cutter. Place 1/2-ounce of filling in the middle and brush the edges with egg wash. Fold the edges up like a taco and seal between your fingers.

2. Crimp edges with a fork and fry the pies at 375°F for about 3 minutes, or until golden brown

Bread Pudding with Rum Sauce
Liberty's Kitchen
New Orleans, LA

10 eggs
1 quart granulated sugar
1 quart half and half
1 Tbsp. vanilla extract
1 Tbsp. ground cinnamon
Pinch of salt
2.5 loaves (30" each) day-old French bread – we use Leidenheimer's

Rum Sauce:
½ lb. light brown sugar
¼ lb. (or 8 Tbsp.) chilled butter- cubed
2 Tbsp. light corn syrup
1 tsp. ground cinnamon
Pinch of salt
½ cup rum
¼ cup cream

Steps for Bread Pudding:

1. Combine all ingredients (except bread) in large mixing bowl and whisk thoroughly.

2. Cut French bread into 1"x1"cubes and place in a 2.5-3 gallon container or pot. 3. Pour the mixture (from step 1) over the cubed bread and mix gently with a long spoon or rubber spatula until bread has absorbed most of the mixture.

4. Cover and place in refrigerator for at least 30 minutes (it can remain in the refrigerator for several days, if needed).

5. Preheat oven to 325 degrees.

6. Spray an aluminum "half-pan" (dimensions at top of page) with a non-stick spray and place a piece of 17"x14" parchment paper inside the pan so that the paper adheres to the pan.

7. Spray the parchment paper to prevent the Bread Pudding from sticking to it.

8. Pour the soaked bread into the pan and press it down so the top is flat.

9. Cover the pan with parchment paper, then cover the parchment paper with foil and crimp the edges of the foil so it holds to the pan. Place pan with bread pudding into another aluminum half pan or place the pan with bread pudding in a larger deep pan with 1 ½ inches of water, so that water reaches half way up the pan. This will prevent the sides and bottom of bread pudding from burning.

10. Place in the oven for 1 hour and 15 minutes.

11. Remove and uncover, then continue to bake an additional 20 minutes until the top is light-to-medium brown.

12. Remove Bread Pudding from oven.

Steps for Rum Sauce (thermometer recommended)

1. Combine brown sugar, corn syrup, cinnamon, and salt into a medium-sized pot (sugar will expand to more than twice its volume when it boils).

2. Add just enough water to the pot to wet the brown sugar.

3. Place the pot on the stove with the flame/heat on high.

4. Stir ingredients in the pot with a long-handled wooden spoon just until all components are homogenized.

5. Boil rapidly until it reaches 240 degrees F (should only take a few minutes).

6. Turn flame/heat to low and slowly stir in chilled, cubed butter.

7. Once the butter is melted, turn flame/heat back to high.

8. When you reach a boil, pour in rum (CAUTION: RUM IS FLAMMABLE).

9. Continue to boil another 2 minutes. Rum should ignite... let it burn itself out.

10. After rum has burned off, add cream (this will reduce the heat).

11. Once the sauce comes back to a boil, remove the pot and pour Rum Sauce over the hot Bread Pudding.

Creole Gumbo
Lil' Dizzy's Café
New Orleans, LA

1¼ pounds seasoning ham
1¼ pounds smoked sausage
1½ pounds chicken pieces
½ pound hot sausage
1½ pounds peeled shrimp
6 to 8 gumbo crabs
1 dozen oysters
2 cups chopped onion
¼ cup chopped garlic
3 green onions, chopped

½ green bell pepper, chopped
2 teaspoons thyme leaves
5 bay leaves
⅔ cup vegetable oil
4 to 5 tablespoons flour
10 cups water
filé powder
salt and pepper
hot cooked rice, for serving

1. Cube ham and slice sausages. Heat oil in an eight to ten-quart pot. Add ham to brown.

2. Add onions and cook until tender. Add chicken and sausages and brown. Add shrimp and other seasonings and cook five minutes.

3. Sprinkle flour over meats and seasonings and stir well.

4. Add water and bring to a simmer. Add salt and pepper to taste.

5. Add gumbo crabs and cook on medium to low fire about 45 minutes. Add oysters and cook five minutes. Turn off heat.

6. Add filé powder (to taste) and stir into gumbo. Serve over cooked rice.
Serves 10 to 12.

Mardi Gras King Cake
Marguerite's Cakes
New Orleans, LA

For the Cake:
8 ounces granulated sugar
8 ounces shortening
2 pounds 4 ounces bread flour
1/2 ounce salt
2 ounces yeast
1 ounce powdered milk

2 cups warm water
4 ounces whole eggs
For the icing:
1 pound powdered sugar
1 teaspoon of your favorite flavoring
(suggested:almond extract)
1/4 cup warm water

1. Use dough hook on low speed to mix all dry ingredients first until blended, then add whole eggs and water, pouring slowly until mixed. Put mixer on medium speed until dough forms a ball. Put a towel over bowl, let rise until double in size. Take out of bowl, cut into two 1- pound sections, roll ash section out long ways, cut in half, sprinkle with cinnamon and sugar mixture on each piece. Roll each piece and twist together. Close ends to make a circle. Put the two cakes on baking sheet and let rise again until double in size. Bake at 350 degrees for 15-20 minutes. Let cool. Mix all icing ingredients until blended. Add water slowly to get a thin consistency. Drizzle over king cake. Sprinkle with purple, green and gold sugar around top of cake while icing is wet.

White Chocolate Bread Pudding with Bananas and Rum Sauce

Mat & Naddie's Restaurant
New Orleans, LA

Bread Pudding:
4½ cups milk
20 tbsp. unsalted butter
1 cup sugar
2 tsp. vanilla extract
1 tsp. freshly grated nutmeg
¼ tsp. kosher salt
12 oz. stale country white bread, cut into ½" cubes (about 8 cups)
6 oz. white chocolate, roughly chopped, plus more for garnish
½ cup toasted slivered almonds
8 eggs

1 cup flour
2 cups panko bread crumbs
Rum Sauce and Bananas:
1½ cups sugar
1 cup heavy cream
4 tbsp. unsalted butter, cubed
2 tbsp. dark rum
½ tsp. fresh lemon juice
½ cup turbinado sugar, such as Sugar In the Raw
4 bananas, halved lengthwise and then halved crosswise

1. Make the bread pudding: Bring 4 cups milk, 16 tbsp. butter, sugar, vanilla, nutmeg, and salt to a simmer in a 4-qt. saucepan over medium-high heat; remove from heat, and let cool for 20 minutes. Combine bread, chocolate, and almonds in a large bowl; set aside. Add 6 eggs to milk mixture, and whisk until smooth. Pour custard over bread mixture, and stir until evenly combined; let sit to soften bread, about 20 minutes. Heat oven to 300°. Pour bread mixture into a 9" × 13" metal baking pan, making sure ingredients are evenly distributed, cover with foil, and bake until set, about 1 hour. Let cool to room temperature, and then refrigerate until chilled, at least 2 hours or overnight.

2. Meanwhile, make rum sauce: Bring sugar and ½ cup water to a boil in a 2-qt. saucepan over high heat, stirring until sugar dissolves; cook, without stirring, until sugar turns into an amber-colored caramel, about 15 minutes. Add cream, butter, rum, and juice, and stir until smooth; set sauce aside.

3. Place flour and bread crumbs in separate shallow dishes; whisk together remaining milk and eggs in a third shallow dish. Unmold bread pudding from pan, and cut into 8 rectangles. Heat 2 tbsp. butter in a 12" skillet over medium heat. Dredge each piece in flour, then coat in the milk mixture, and finally coat in bread crumbs. Add 4 pieces to skillet, and cook, turning once, until golden brown on both sides, about 6 minutes. Transfer to paper towels to drain briefly; repeat with remaining butter and pieces. While pudding is still hot, top each with a chunk of white chocolate.

4. To serve, place turbinado sugar on a plate, and dip the flat cut-side of each banana quarter in sugar to cover completely; place sugar-side up on a foil-lined baking sheet. Using a handheld blowtorch or the broiler, heat sugar until melted and caramelized, about 6 minutes if broiling; set aside. Pour rum sauce in the middle of 8 serving plates, and place 1 piece pudding in the center of each; place 2 brûléed banana quarters on either side of the bread pudding.

Catfish Po-Boy
Middendorf's
New Orleans, LA

For the Catfish Po Boy:
Oil for frying
8 5-6 inch catfish filets
4 cups fine corn meal (if too course, process until fine in a food processor)
Bowl of slightly salted water
Tartar sauce (ingredients below)
Cocktail sauce (ingredients below)
4 8-inch lengths of New Orleans French bread or Hoagie roll

Optional condiments: dill pickle chips, lettuce, tomatoes, hot sauce

For the Cocktail Sauce:
1/2 cup chili sauce
1/2 cup ketchup
1 tablespoon prepared horseradish
Dash Worcestershire sauce

For the Tartar Sauce:
1 cup mayonnaise
1 tablespoon finely chopped dill pickle
1 tablespoon minced onion
2 tablespoons lemon juice
1 tablespoon finely chopped, pitted green olives
1 clove finely minced garlic

1. Heat oil in a deep fat fryer to 350 degrees.

2. One at a time, dip the filets in the salted water then quickly dredge in the cornmeal. 3. Carefully lat the filet in the oil to fry. Fry in small batches and do not crowd the filets. Fry until crispy. Do not worry about overcooking.

4. Drain catfish on paper towels.

5. Use two filets for each sandwich.

6. Slice the lengths of bread horizontally and brush each inside part with butter.

7. Toast under a broiler until light brown. Spread tartar sauce on one side of the bread and cocktail sauce on the other.

8. Top with hot catfish filets.

9. If desired, add sliced dill pickles, finely shredded lettuce, and ripe sliced Creole tomatoes. A couple of drops of Louisiana hot sauce are also optional.

10. Cut each sandwich in half. Serve with tangy cole slaw and a cold Barq's root beer. Serves 4.

11. To prepare the Cocktail Sauce :Mix all ingredients. Chill.

12. To Prepare the Tartar Sauce :Mix all ingredients. Chill.

Barbequed Shrimp
Mr. B.'s Bistro
New Orleans, LA

16 jumbo shrimp (12 per pound, about 1 1/2 pounds), with heads and unpeeled
1/2 cup Worcestershire sauce
2 tablespoons fresh lemon juice (about 2 lemons)
2 teaspoons ground black pepper
2 teaspoons cracked black pepper
2 teaspoons Creole seasoning
1 teaspoon minced garlic
1 1/2 cups (3 sticks) cold unsalted butter, cubed
French bread as accompaniment

1. In a large skillet combine shrimp, Worcestershire, lemon juice, black peppers, Creole seasoning, and garlic and cook over moderately high heat until shrimp turn pink, about 1 minute on each side. Reduce heat to moderate and stir in butter, a few cubes at a time, stirring constantly and adding more only when butter is melted. Remove skillet from heat. Place shrimp in a bowl and pour sauce over top. Serve with French bread for dipping.

Pan Roasted Oysters
Muriel's
New Orleans, LA

3 oz. heavy cream
1 oz. oyster water
1 oz. mushrooms, quartered
½ oz. leeks, cleaned and sliced

1 sprig fresh thyme, picked
1 Tbl. Canola oil
1 tsp. unsalted butter
3-5 shucked oysters

1. In a small saute pan over medium-high heat add oil. When oil is hot, add mushrooms and saute until lightly browned. Add leeks, and continue to cook until softened. Pour in heavy cream and oyster water and reduce by half. Add oysters and the thyme and cook until oysters start to curl up. Turn off heat and add butter and stir until incorporated. Season with salt and pepper.

Black-Eyed Pea Battered Shrimp
Nicholls State University-John Folse
New Orleans, LA

36 (16–20 count) shrimp, head-on
3/4 cup black-eyed peas, cooked
1/4 cup diced onion
1 tablespoon minced garlic
1/8 teaspoon ground ginger
Creole seasoning to taste
salt and black pepper to taste

granulated garlic to taste
2 large eggs
1/4 cup olive oil
1 1/4 cups beer
Louisiana hot sauce to taste
2 cups flour
1 quart vegetable oil

1. Peel shells from tail of shrimp, being careful not to remove head. Devein shrimp then set aside.

2. In a food processor, combine black-eyed peas, onion, minced garlic, ginger, Creole seasoning, salt, pepper and granulated garlic. Blend on high speed 2–3 minutes or until peas are coarsely chopped.

3. Add eggs, olive oil, beer and hot sauce. Blend 1–2 minutes or until puréed. Add flour and blend 1–2 minutes. Pour black-eyed pea batter into a ceramic bowl then set aside.

4. In a large cast iron pot or a home-style electric fryer such as a FryDaddy®, heat 3 inches of oil to 350°F according to manufacturer's directions. Dip shrimp bodies (not heads) into batter and allow all excess to drain. Gently place shrimp into deep-fryer and cook until golden brown and partially floating. Remove from oil and drain.

5. Serve hot with your favorite dipping sauce.

{ *In 1872, the official colors of Mardi Gras were chosen based on an honored visitor to New Orleans: Russian Grand Duke Alexis Romanoff. The purple stands for justice, the green for faith, and the gold for power.* }

Roast Beef Po-Boys
Parkway Bakery & Tavern
New Orleans, LA

5-pound beef chuck roast
Garlic powder
Onion powder
Salt and pepper
2 tablespoons vegetable oil
1 can beef stock
1 can cream of mushroom soup
2 tablespoons Kitchen Bouquet
3 large carrots, peeled, cut in 3-inch pieces
1 large or two small onions, cut in chunks
3 stalks celery, cut in 3-inch pieces

2 bay leaves
1 teaspoon powdered thyme or thyme leaves

For po-boys:
1 or 2 loaves New Orleans French bread, such as Reising or Leidenheimer, cut in 6-inch segments
2 large tomatoes, thinly sliced
Shredded iceberg lettuce
Dill pickles, drained
Mayonnaise

1. Lavishly sprinkle the roast with garlic powder, onion powder, salt and pepper, and rub it into both sides. Heat oil in your heaviest pot with a lid, such as a Magnalite or cast iron pan. Add the roast. Over high heat, sear it on both sides until well browned, turning once with tongs and a heavy spatula.

2. Preheat oven to 325 degrees. Mix in a medium bowl the beef stock, cream of mushroom soup and Kitchen Bouquet, whisking if necessary to break up lumps. Put the vegetables beside and under the roast. Pour the beef stock mixture over all and make sure everything is covered by the liquid.

3. Put the lid on the pot and put it in the oven. After two hours, check to see if the meat needs to be rearranged in the liquid to be completely covered. Put the lid back on and return to the oven. After another hour, remove and use a fork to check the consistency of the roast. If it doesn't shred easily, return to the oven for another hour. Total cooking time should be three or four hours.

4. Remove from the oven when fork-tender. Remove the meat to a refrigerator container, leaving the liquid in the pot. Cover and refrigerate the meat.

5. Remove bay leaves. Set a sieve over a large bowl, and ladle the liquid through the sieve. Add the vegetables to the sieve, and use the back of a ladle or large spoon to press the tender carrots through the sieve into the sauce. Press as much of the vegetables through the sieve as possible. Taste and season with salt and pepper if necessary. Put the sauce into another refrigerator container; cover and refrigerate.

6. The next day, remove the meat to a cutting board. Use a very sharp knife to slice the roast as thinly as possible, about 1/8-inch. Remove fat from the top of the sauce and discard. Pour the sauce into a large saucepan, and add the slices to the sauce. Reheat over medium heat.

7. Cut French bread horizontally into two pieces, and toast until interiors are just browned. Lay the slices flat on a work surface. Cover one side with iceberg lettuce, then a layer of tomatoes, then pickles. Smear mayonnaise evenly on the other half, then generously layer on the warmed meat. Top with a ladle of gravy, then carefully press the two slices together.

Barbeque Shrimp
Pascal's Manale Restaurant
New Orleans, LA

Shrimp:
1 pound (21-25 count) shrimp, heads removed
5 teaspoons Manale Spice (recipe follows)
1/2 teaspoon minced garlic
1/2 teaspoon Worcestershire sauce
1/4 teaspoon Louisiana hot sauce
3/4 cup extra virgin olive oil
1/2 cup white wine
1 tablespoon unsalted butter
French bread for serving

Manale Spice:
4 tablespoons black pepper
1/4 teaspoon cayenne pepper
1 teaspoon paprika
1 teaspoon salt
1 teaspoon thyme
1 teaspoon oregano
1 teaspoon basil

1. Wash shrimp and pat dry. Put shrimp in a large skillet over high heat and add Manale Spice, garlic, Worcestershire sauce and hot sauce, stirring constantly. Pour olive oil over shrimp, then add white wine. Stir to blend all ingredients thoroughly.

2. Continue cooking over high heat for 8 minutes, stirring frequently. Add butter, and cook an additional 2 minutes until butter is thoroughly melted and blended in. Be careful not to overcook shrimp or they will become tough. Serve with French bread for dipping in sauce.

Manale Spice:

1. Combine all ingredients thoroughly and store in a dry, airtight container.

Skewered Shrimp with Cilantro Coconut Dipping Sauce
Refuel Café
New Orleans, LA

20 large Louisiana shrimp (16-20 count)
2 14-ounce cans cream of coconut, in all
4 ounces Malibu rum, in all
salt and pepper, to taste
10 4-inch knotted bamboo skewers
1/4 cup toasted shredded coconut
1/4 cup pineapple juice
4 tablespoons chopped fresh cilantro

1. Soak skewers in water for 30 minutes.

2. Peel and devein shrimp.

3. Sprinkle with salt and pepper.

4. Mix 1 can cream of coconut and 3 ounces rum and combine with shrimp to marinate.

5. Refrigerate for at least 2 hours.

6. Place 2 shrimp on each skewer and grill until shrimp are opaque and firm.

7. Plate shrimp and dust lightly with toasted coconut.

8. Mix remaining can cream of coconut, pineapple juice, rum, and cilantro and serve as a dipping sauce for shrimp.

9. Garnish with cilantro sprigs.

Crawfish and Andouille Grits
Restaurant August
New Orleans, LA

White Grits:
4 cups water
1 teaspoon salt
1 cup Anson Mill white stone-ground organic grits
1/2 cup Mascarpone cheese
2 tablespoons butter

Crawfish Stock:
1 rib celery, quartered
1 carrot, peeled and quartered
1 onion, peeled and quartered
1 sprig thyme
1 head garlic, split in half
2 pounds Louisiana crawfish shells
1 gallon water (or just enough to cover shells)

Sautéed Crawfish and Sauce:
2 tablespoons extra virgin olive oil
30 large Louisiana crawfish tails
Creole spice, to taste
salt, to taste
6 tablespoons Jacob's Andouille sausage, diced small
1 tablespoon minced garlic
1 tablespoon minced shallot
2 tablespoons small diced Piquillo pepper
1 tablespoon chopped thyme
1 quart crawfish stock
2 tablespoons unsalted butter
2 cups diced tomatoes
1 tablespoon chopped chives
1 teaspoon fresh lemon juice
1/2 cup chervil pluches (small 3-leafed sprigs of chervil), for garnish

White Grits:

1. Bring the water to a boil and lightly season with salt. Add the grits while stirring rapidly and reduce heat to low. Simmer the grits for about 20 minutes, stirring constantly to prevent them from sticking to the bottom of the pot.
2. To finish, turn off heat and stir in butter and Mascarpone cheese.

Crawfish Stock:

1. To a large pot, add celery, carrot, onion, thyme, garlic, shells, and just enough water to cover the other ingredients. Simmer on low for 1 hour, skimming the fat off throughout the hour.
2. Strain and reserve liquid in refrigerator.

Sautéed Crawfish and Sauce:

1. Heat a large pan over medium heat and add the olive oil. Season the crawfish tails with Creole spice and salt and sauté until they start to brown but are not cooked all the way through. Remove the crawfish and hold on the side.
2. To the pan add the Andouille sausage, garlic, shallot, Piquillo pepper, and thyme, and sauté until they become aromatic. Add the stock and bring to a low simmer. Stir in the butter and reduce until thickened. Add crawfish back to the pot and cook through.
3. Finish with tomatoes, chives, and lemon juice.

Serve:

1. For each serving, place 4 tablespoons of grits in the middle of a large bowl.
2. Divide the crawfish evenly atop the grits and spoon the sauce around to fill in the negative space.
3. Garnish with fresh chervil.

Crab Pound Cake
Restaurant Revolution
New Orleans, LA

2 cups corn flour
2 cups all-purpose flour
1 3/4 cups sugar
7 whole eggs
1 cup sour cream
1/2 tablespoon salt
3/4 pound butter (melted)
3/4 tablespoon baking powder
Port Salut Icing
1/2 quart heavy cream
1/2 quart half and half
1/4 ounce fresh thyme

1 garlic clove minced
1 shallot diced
1 bay leaf
6 ounces port salut cheese
1/2 teaspoon butter
2 ounces brandy
8 ounces crab meat
salt and pepper to taste
Pepper Sprinkles
1 green bell pepper, very small diced
1 red bell pepper, very small diced
1 yellow bell pepper, very small diced

1. Preheat your oven to 300°F.

2. Whisk together sugar and eggs. Sift all other dry ingredients. Combine dry ingredients with egg mixture. Add melted butter to strained mixture. Place mixture in a large square cake pan (9" or 10") with tall sides, filling pan only half full. Bake for 25 to 30 minutes or until toothpick can be removed from the center of the cake clean.

Port Salut Icing

1. Sauté garlic and shallots in butter until shallots are translucent. Deglaze with brandy and ignite. Add remaining ingredients except port salut. Cook on medium low heat until mixture is reduced by half. Whisk in the port salut. Allow to cook for five minutes or until cheese is thoroughly combined. Remove from heat and purée. Strain through mesh strainer. Add picked crab meat to mixture and season to taste.

2. Pour over a small piece of pound cake. Top with pepper sprinkles to taste (recipe below).

Pepper Sprinkles

1. Place on a non-stick pan and place in the oven, with just the pilot light, on over night to dry out. If you do not have a gas stove you can cook in electric oven at 140°F or the lowest setting on the oven for 30 minutes.

2. Check peppers for dryness, cook longer if not dried out completely.

Grilled Mahi-Mahi with Escabeche Sauce
RioMar
New Orleans, LA

1 medium red pepper, sliced thinly
1 medium green pepper, sliced thinly
1 small red onion, sliced thinly
2 garlic cloves, sliced thinly
6 pitted black olives, sliced
6 pitted green olives, sliced
3 tablespoons capers
1/4 cup brine from olives

1 tablespoon chopped flat-leaf parsley
1/2 cup tomato juice
3 tablespoons sherry vinegar
3 tablespoons extra-virgin olive oil
4 (8-ounce) pieces mahi-mahi or similar fish
1/2 teaspoon salt
1/2 teaspoon freshly ground pepper

1. Stir together first 12 ingredients in a bowl, and refrigerate until needed.

2. Season fish on both sides with salt and pepper. Coat a grill tray with cooking spray, and place on grill rack. Heat, covered with grill lid, over hot coals (400°-500°) for 10 minutes. Place fish on tray, and grill over medium-high heat 8 minutes on each side. Serve fish hot, topped with cold or room-temperature sauce.

Ramos Gin Fizz
Roosevelt Hotel
New Orleans, LA

2 oz. gin (London Dry or Old Tom)
1 oz. heavy cream
1 oz. simple syrup
1/2 oz. fresh squeezed lemon juice

1/2 oz. fresh squeezed lime juice
1 egg white
3 dashes orange blossom water
1 drop vanilla extract, (optional)

1. Combine ingredients and dry shake for 10 seconds without ice.

2. Add several small to medium sized ice cubes and shake hard for several minutes.

3. Continue shaking as long as you are able and until you can no longer hear the ice inside.

4. Pour foamy contents into a chilled Collins glass and slowly top with soda to rise the head.

5. A straw is optional, but when placed, it should stand on its own in the center of the drink.

Grilled Bronzini
Salu
New Orleans, LA

2 bronzini, gutted. fins and gills removed
2 lemons. juiced and zested
2 lemons. split in half and sliced into
half-moons
8 thyme sprigs
8 parsley sprigs
4 T extra-virgin olive oil
Salt and pepper as desired

Thyme Vinaigrette
2 T thyme, dried
1/2 cup red wine vinegar
1 1/2 cup extra-virgin olive oil
Salt and pepper as desired

1. Combine lemons, herbs, and oil in a large bowl. Stuff the fish with the lemon herb mix dividing the mix evenly between the two fish. Pour the remaining liquid over the fish and refrigerate for 30 minutes. Place the fish on the hottest part of your grill until the skin releases from the grates, then flip and repeat.

Thyme Vinaigrette:

1. Combine all ingredients in a bowl and whisk until well combined. Drizzle over the grilled fish. The vinaigrette will separate as it sits. Whisk it back together at your leisure.

Sazerac
Sazerac Coffee House
New Orleans, LA

½ tsp. sugar
2 oz. Sazerac rye
2 dashes Peychaud's bitters

1 lemon peel twist
8 drops Herbsaint liqueur

1. Dissolve sugar in 1 tsp. water in a shaker; fill with ice. Add rye, bitters, and peel; stir to chill. Swirl Herb-saint in a rocks glass; discard. Strain rye mixture into glass. Serve alongside ice water.

Welsh Rarebit
St. James Cheese Company
New Orleans, LA

3 Egg Yolks,
50 ml Brown Ale
1 tbsp Dijon Mustard
1 tbsp Worcestershire Sauce

200 g Cheddar cheese
3 Shallots, finely chopped,
Sliced and toasted bread

1. Mix all the ingredients together in a bowl. Preheat the broiler. Toast the bread on both sides. Spread a layer of the cheese mix on top, quite thickly, and broil until brown and blistered. Serve immediately.

Bananas Foster French Toast
Stella!
New Orleans, LA

Spicy Candied Walnuts:
1 cup walnuts, toasted
1 cup confectioner's sugar
1 tablespoon cinnamon
¼ teaspoon cayenne pepper
¼ teaspoon nutmeg
3 tablespoons granulated sugar
½ teaspoon kosher salt
1 quart boiling water
1 quart peanut oil
Crispy Plantains:
1 green plantain
1 quart peanut oil (above)
French Toast:
2 eggs
1 cup half and half
1 French baguette loaf or other French-style

bread loaf, sliced
½ cup (1 stick) unsalted butter
1 tablespoon granulated sugar
¼ teaspoon nutmeg
1 teaspoon cinnamon
Bananas Foster Sauce:
½ pound (2 sticks) unsalted butter
2 teaspoons cinnamon
2 cups light brown sugar
½ ounce banana liquor
½ teaspoon nutmeg
2 bananas, peeled and sliced into thin disks
1 quart vanilla bean ice cream
2 ounces light rum
Confectioner's sugar for dusting
4 mint sprigs

1. To make the candied walnuts, place a wire rack on a baking sheet. Place the toasted nuts in a hand-held strainer and submerse in the boiling water for 30 seconds. Remove and blot dry on a towel. Toss in a bowl with the confectioner's sugar. Heat the peanut oil in a deep-fryer or deep saucepan until almost smoking. Working with one half of the nuts at a time, put the nuts back in the strainer and lower into the hot oil for 5 seconds; remove and pour out onto the wire rack. Mix the cinnamon, nutmeg, cayenne, sugar and salt together and dust over the hot walnuts. Let cool. Set the oil aside.

2. To prepare the plantains, peel the plantain and slice lengthwise into thin strips on a mandoline or V-slicer. Reheat the peanut oil to 370 degrees F. Drop the plantain slices into the hot oil and fry until they become crisp and float to the top. Remove with a slotted spoon or wire skimmer and drain on paper towels. Set aside until ready to use.

3. To prepare the French toast, place a wire rack on a baking sheet. Mix the eggs and half and half in a shallow bowl, whisking slightly to break up the eggs. Soak the bread slices in the egg mixture. Melt the butter in a large nonstick sauté pan or skillet over medium-high heat. Sauté the soaked bread slices in the butter until deep golden brown on both sides. Lift with tongs and place on the wire rack. Mix the cinnamon, nutmeg and sugar, dust over the bread. Set aside and keep warm.

4. To prepare the Sauce, Melt the butter, brown sugar, cinnamon and nutmeg in a small sauté pan or skillet over medium heat. When bubbling hot, add the liqueur and rum, avert your face and ignite with a match; shake the pan until the alcohol is burned off and the flame dies down. Add the banana slices and toss until coated. Set aside; keep warm.

Boiled Beef Brisket
Tujague's Restaurant
New Orleans, LA

6-7 pounds choice brisket
2 onions, quartered
1½ ribs of celery, quartered
1 head of garlic, peeled
1 bay leaf
1 Tablespoon salt
15 black peppercorns

2 green onions, quartered
1 carrot, quartered
1 bell pepper, quartered
Sauce
1 Cup ketchup
½ Cup horseradish
¼ Cup creole mustard

1. Place the brisket in a large soup pot, cover with cold water, add all the ingredients and simmer for 3-4 hours until beef is tender.

2. Remove beef and slice. For vegetable soup, skim and strain the stock.

3. Add 3 tablespoons tomato paste, 2 whole tomatoes sliced, and your favorite vegetables.

4. Cook until tender and serve.

Fried Green Tomatoes With Shrimp Rémoulade
Upperline
New Orleans, LA

1 large egg
1 cup buttermilk
1 cup yellow cornmeal
1/2 teaspoon salt, or to taste
1/4 teaspoon freshly ground pepper, to taste
8 (1/2-inch-thick) slices all-green tomatoes
(about 2 medium tomatoes)
6 tablespoons vegetable oil
24 medium shrimp (about 1/2 pound)
peeled, cooked, and chilled
1 cup Remoulade Sauce
Remoulade Sauce
1/2 cup Creole mustard
2 tablespoons ketchup
1 teaspoon Worcestershire sauce

2 teaspoons prepared horseradish
1 medium garlic clove, finely chopped
(about 1 teaspoon)
1 teaspoon freshly squeezed lemon juice
1 1/2 teaspoons paprika
1/4 teaspoon ground white pepper
1/8 teaspoon finely ground black pepper
1/8 teaspoon cayenne pepper, or to taste
Salt, to taste
2 tablespoons olive oil
1/4 cup finely chopped celery ribs, with leaves
1 1/2 teaspoons finely chopped fresh parsley
1 tablespoon grated white or yellow onion
1 tablespoon finely chopped green onion top
Hot sauce, if desired

1. Whisk together egg and buttermilk in a medium bowl. Combine cornmeal, salt, and pepper in a shallow dish. Dip tomato slices in egg mixture, then coat with seasoned cornmeal.

2. Heat oil in a large sauté pan over medium heat. Place tomato slices in pan in a single layer, and cook until golden brown on bottom, about 3 minutes. Flip and brown other side, about 3 minutes more. Interior should be cooked through but not mushy.

3. Place 2 tomato slices on each of 4 serving plates and top each slice with 3 shrimp. Spoon 1 1/2 tablespoons Remoulade Sauce over each slice, and garnish, if desired. Serve immediately.

Remoulade Sauce:

1. Stir together first 10 ingredients in a bowl. Taste and add salt as needed.

2. While whisking mixture, add olive oil in a slow stream. Add celery and next 3 ingredients; stir well. Add a few drops of hot sauce if spicier flavor is desired. Sauce should be spicy and tangy. Cover and refrigerate up to 3 weeks.

Jambalaya
The Old Coffee Pot
New Orleans, LA

1 Tbsp. unsalted butter
1 1/2 cups diced Andouille sausage
1/4 cup diced onion
1/4 cup diced bell pepper
1/4 cup diced celery
1 clove garlic, chopped

1 1/2 cups diced chicken
2 cups parboiled long grain white rice
2 cups tomato sauce
2 cups chicken or beef stock
salt and freshly ground black pepper

1. Melt the butter in a medium pot over medium heat.

2. Add the sausage, onions, bell peppers, celery, and garlic. Sauté until the sausage begins to brown (5 to 8 minutes).

3. Add the chicken and allow to brown on all sides.

4. Add rice, tomato sauce, stock. Add salt and pepper to taste.

5. Bring to a boil, then reduce to a simmer and cook, uncovered, until the rice is tender (20 to 25 minutes,) stirring occasionally.

6. Sit jambalaya aside until later, but keep it warm.

Fleur de Lis Chicken
The Old Coffee Pot
New Orleans, LA

4 oz. unsalted butter
½ cup white wine
½ cup heavy cream
1 tsp. lemon juice
4 chicken breasts
8 large butterflied shrimp

6 oz. crab meat
2 cloves garlic, chopped
1 egg
1 oz. remoulade sauce
1 oz. bread crumbs
Salt, pepper to taste

1. In a mixing bowl add crab, garlic, egg, remoulade and salt and pepper. Gently mix together.

2. Add bread crumbs and make four small balls. Pat down crab balls to create crab cakes.

3. Season chicken breast with Creole seasoning (or use salt & pepper) and sauté on medium high heat for about 3 min on each side (until internal temp reaches 165 degrees). Keep warm in a low oven.

4. Sauté crab cakes. Remove from pan. Then sauté shrimp in same pan. Remove from the pan. Place crab & shrimp in low oven with the chicken to keep warm.

5. Buerre blanc sauce: In the same pan, add white wine and scrape the bottom of the pan to deglaze the pan, getting all the bits stuck in the pan to add flavor.

6. Add cream and lemon juice, reduce by half.

7. Add butter and mix constantly until a sauce is made. Keep warm. Prepare to plate the meal.

{ *The total mileage of canals both above and below ground in New Orleans exceeds that of Venice in Italy.* }

Crab Risotto with Saffron
The Irish House
New Orleans

2 1/2 cups rice
1/2 cup finely chopped white onion cup
unsalted butter
1/2 cups crab stock
2 1/2 cups white wine

1/2 cup freshly grated Italian Parmesan
8 ounces jumbo lump crabmeat
1 tablespoon of saffron
salt, to taste
pepper, to taste

1. In a large non-stick pan cook the onions in 1/4 cup butter until they're translucent being careful not to brown them. When the onions are ready add the rice, combine it well with the onions and butter, and toast it for about 2 to 3 minutes at high heat.

2. Add 2 cups of wine and mix well until it evaporates. Use a good white wine. Add about 2 cups of stock and reduce the heat to medium, stirring frequently. Once absorbed add saffron. Continue adding broth in the same quantity mixing frequently. Continue doing so until the rice is nearly cooked. When the rice is almost cooked (it should be 15 to 20 minutes) add 1/4 cup butter and the Parmesan.

3. Remove from the stove, cover the pan with the lid and let it stand for few minutes. Season with salt and pepper.

4. Serve hot.

Green Bean Casserole
The Old Coffee Pot
New Orleans, LA

2 oz. unsalted butter
2 oz. rice flour or all-purpose flour
1 pound green beans(fresh or frozen)
1/4 cup diced onion
1/4 cup diced bell pepper
2 cups sliced cremini mushroom

2 cloves garlic, chopped
1 pint heavy cream
2 oz. Cream Sherry
Salt and pepper to taste
2 oz. parmesan cheese

1. Pre-heat oven to 400 degrees.

2. Melt butter in a medium pot over medium heat.

3. Add flour and whisk until fully incorporated with the butter which creates a roux.

4. Add onion, bell pepper, mushrooms, and green beans. Sauté for 2-3 min.

5. Add garlic, heavy cream, cream sherry, salt and pepper (to taste) and cook until it begins to thicken. 7. Pour into a baking pan and top with parmesan cheese.

6. Place in oven at 400 degrees until cheese begins to melt. (approx. 5 min.) Keep warm in a low oven.

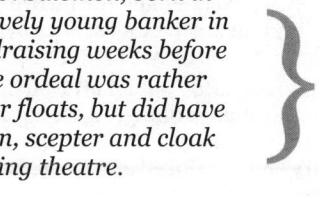

The first king of Rex in 1872 was Louis J. Salomon, born in 1839. Louis J., the first Rex, was a relatively young banker in 1872 who had been put in charge of fundraising weeks before the first Rex parade in 1872. The whole ordeal was rather hastily put together. Rex had no queen or floats, but did have some marching bands. Salomon's crown, scepter and cloak were all borrowed from an acting theatre.

Sylvain's Collard Bourbon Soup
Sylvain's
New Orleans, LA

6 slices good quality bacon, diced
1 large onion, small diced
4 cloves garlic, minced
1 pound collard greens, washed thoroughly
and chopped
Salt and freshly ground black pepper
1/4 cup white wine

1/2 cup bourbon
3 quarts pork or chicken stock
4 bay leaves
1/2 teaspoon red pepper flakes
3 cups cooked black-eyed peas
1-1/2 teaspoons fresh thyme leaves
1 ounce Worcestershire

1. Slowly render the bacon in large, heavy soup pot, until crispy. Add the onion and garlic and cook over medium heat until fragrant and softened.

2. Add the washed collards to the pot and season with salt and pepper. When the collards begin to wilt in the bacon fat, add white wine and bourbon and bring the soup to a simmer. Add the stock, red pepper flakes and bay leaves.

3. Return soup to a simmer; simmer until collards are soft, about 40 minutes. Add the black-eyed peas, thyme and Worcestershire. Taste and adjust the salt and pepper levels, if needed. Serve hot.

Tourtiere Creole
The Grill Room at Windsor Court
New Orleans, LA

3 lbs. ground pork
1 large yellow onion
1 bell pepper
4 ribs celery
4 cloves garlic
1 chili pepper
½ cup white wine
2 Tbsp. flour
2 qts. chicken or pork stock

1 Tbsp. chopped mint
1 Tbsp. chopped sage
1 Tbsp. chopped Italian parsley
3 Tbsp. chopped green onions
12 Louisiana oysters, shucked
Salt, pepper, cayenne to taste
1/3 recipe Puff Dough (recipe follows)
1 bunch watercress

1. For the Filling: In a wide shallow pot or rondeau, render Pork over medium high heat, stirring frequently until pork is uniformly golden brown. Use a slotted spoon to lift out render pork and set aside on paper towels. Add onion, bell pepper, and celery to pan and sauté while using a wooden spoon to scrape brown bits from the bottom of the pan until vegetables are lightly caramelized. Add garlic and chili pepper. Continue to sauté for about one more minute. Return pork to the pan. Deglaze with white wine. Cook until wine is completely evaporated, about five minutes. Add flour. Stir in flour thoroughly. Cook until flour is toasted to a blonde color. Add stock slowly while stirring vigorously. Continue to stir frequently until the mixture boils. Reduce heat to a simmer and cook slowly until pork is meltingly tender and the mixture is quite thick, about two hours. Stir in mint, sage, parsley, and green onions. Season the mixture to taste with salt, pepper and cayenne. Set aside to cool slightly.

2. To Finish: Roll out a Puff Dough to 1/4" thick. Cut into an 11" circle. Fill a 9" cast iron skillet with pork filling. Scatter oysters amongst the filling. Place pastry dish over skillet push with egg wash and cut away excess. Bake at 350 degrees for 45 minutes or until pastry is fully cooked and filling is bubbling. Allow to cool slightly. Garnish with watercress. Serve.

Coca-Cola Fried Chicken
Willie Mae's Scotch House
New Orleans, LA

Brining Chicken:
12 chicken thighs, bone-in, skin-on
4 cups Coca-Cola
1 tsp liquid smoke (optional)
2 tbsp Worcestershire sauce
1 tbsp Tabasco sauce
3 tbsp coarse salt
3 tbsp freshly ground black pepper
Batter:
1 large egg
3/4 cup peanut oil
2 tsp baking powder
2 tbsp coarse salt
4 tsp freshly ground black pepper

1 tbsp cayenne pepper
1 tbsp onion powder
1 tbsp garlic powder
2 cups all-purpose flour
Frying Chicken:
peanut oil and lard
coarse salt and freshly ground black pepper
Pickle-Garlic Relish:
1 cup fresh flat-leaf parsley
1 cup dill-pickle chips, plus a little pickle juice if desired
3 tbsp minced garlic

To brine the chicken:

1. Rinse the chicken, drain, and set aside.

2. Combine all the remaining brining ingredients in a large bowl, stirring until the salt dissolves. Put the chicken in the brine, cover, and marinate, refrigerated, for 4 hours.

To make the batter:

1. Whisk the egg well in a stainless steel bowl and add the peanut oil and 2 1/2 cups water. In a separate bowl, combine all the remaining batter ingredients, then add the dry mixture to the egg mixture, whisking slowly so the batter doesn't clump.

To fry the chicken:

1. Fill a large cast-iron skillet halfway with equal amounts of peanut oil and lard. Slowly bring the temperature to 375°F. (Use a deep-fat thermometer.)

2. While the oil is heating, remove the chicken from the brine and place in a colander in the sink. Once the chicken has drained, pat it dry with paper towels (a critical step) and season with salt and pepper. Dip the chicken in the batter and place it (carefully) in the hot oil. Adjust the heat, as the chicken will bring the oil temperature down dramatically—you want it back up to just above 350°F. Turn the chicken regularly using tongs to prevent burning. After 8 or 9 minutes, remove a piece, prick it to the bone with a fork, and mash it. If the juices run clear, it's done. Continue cooking if necessary.

To make the pickle garlic relish:

1. Finely chop and combine all the relish ingredients.

2. Serve with the chicken. Cover any leftovers with a dish towel and leave out at room temperature (or in the fridge, if you must, although my grandmother never did). This keeps it crisp.